# Responses to 101 Questions about Feminism

*Denise Lardner Carmody*

PAULIST PRESS
New York/Mahwah

Library of Congress Cataloging-in-Publication Data

Carmody, Denise Lardner, 1935–
    Responses to 101 questions about feminism/Denise Lardner Carmody.
        p.  cm.
    Includes index.
    ISBN 0-8091-3438-1 (pbk.)
    1. Women in Christianity.  2. Woman (Christian theology)  3. Feminism
—Religious aspects—Christianity.  I. Title.  II. Title: Responses to one hundred one questions about feminism.  III. Title: Responses to one hundred and one questions about feminism.
BV639.W7C327 1994
261.8'3442—dc20                                                               93-34709
                                                                                          CIP

Published by Paulist Press
997 Macarthur Boulevard
Mahwah, N.J. 07430

Printed and bound in the United States of America

# CONTENTS

## THE 101 QUESTIONS AND RESPONSES

*Part I: Definitions and Orientations*

# Contents

*Part II: God and Religion*

*Part V: The Church and Feminist Spirituality*

# Contents

FOR ALICIA THESING

# INTRODUCTION

This book appears in a series intended for the general reader. Ideally it offers an inviting, balanced treatment of its topic, through the format of questions and answers. I am pleased to present a study of feminism in this way. Often students and people attending lectures have asked me discrete questions about feminism. In answering, more than once I have felt frustrated, because I've sensed that three or four related questions begged answering, if the person were to get full satisfaction. Thus having the leisure to deal with 101 questions has been gratifying. No doubt many other questions still remain, but at least I've been able to deal with some of the most vexing and recurrent.

My "feminism" is of the unexceptionable variety that simply seeks the equality of women with men. I have no explosive, angry, radical agenda. In Christian perspective, I seek merely the share of humanity promised in Genesis, where God creates human beings male and female. Each is the image of God, bearing the divine imprint deeply. Each is also flawed and has reason to blush. Without cooperation, the sexes cannot be fruitful, multiply, fill the earth or guide it well. Without mutual love and respect, they cannot comprise the rich expression of God, little less than the angels, that Jesus promised in preaching the dawning of God's reign.

By a dozen titles, then, Christians should be feminists. If they cannot champion the full humanity of their daughters, as well as their sons, where has their faith left them? Certainly, championing the full humanity, the equal opportunity, of one's daughters can lead to some melancholy vistas, but sadness is not the whole story. Everywhere today women are both doing remarkable things and hoping for things still more remarkable. All over the world the proposition that the dignity and potential of women does credit to our half of the race rings out self-evidently. Observers only need eyes to see with, ears to hear. I conceive of this book as simply a little more evidence for this proposition, couched with a special concern for the followers of the Christ who was a special favorite of both Martha and Mary.

*Part I:*

---

# DEFINITIONS AND ORIENTATIONS

## 1. What ought the word "feminism" to signify?

Different authors impose different meanings. I believe the word should mean "commitment to the equality of women with men." Here "commitment" indicates a choice. One decides to be an advocate of justice toward women. One chooses to speak and act so that women receive treatments—economic, political, religious, and other—on a par with the treatments that men receive. Never mind that the word "equality" is not easy to explain in all particulars. Never mind that women and men are irreducibly different in some aspects of their biology, and that everywhere one finds women and men formed by at least slightly different sets of psychological, sociological, and cultural expectations. One can still discern or intuit what "equality" means with sufficient clarity to know when a woman is not being treated fairly—when a sexual injustice is occurring.

For example, a woman who does the same job as a man but receives significantly less compensation is probably being treated unjustly. In her case, one has to suspect that equality is not being served. Some particulars may force us to place some nuance on this judgment. The man may have greater seniority in the job or win more plaudits for his performance. But, apart from given particulars such as these, we are right to expect that similar work should receive similar compensation. Equally, we are right to judge that a woman doing the same job as a man but receiving markedly less pay is not receiving equal or fair treatment.

What is feminist about a negative reaction to such a situation is the sense that this is not an isolated occurrence, and that women regularly need support and championing. If one perceives that women regularly receive less recompense, or respect, or applause than men, one ought to incline to the women's side, the same as one would incline to the side of children or handicapped people, if one found them not being treated fairly. Feminism is the commitment to help women receive fair treatment. It involves political action to rectify the legal and social structural barriers to provide justice for

5

women. It also involves educating oneself and others in order to remove the intellectual and emotional barriers that contribute to perceptions that women are not the equals of men in their humanness.

## 2. What is "radical feminism"?

Once again, definitions vary, but the general meaning of this term is a feminism—an advocacy of the rights and virtues of women—that calls the preferring of men to women a great (perhaps the greatest) evil. Radical feminists tend to prefer "women's ways" to those of men. Women's ways usually turn out to be tendencies to cooperate rather than compete, discuss rather than fight, think of reality as interlocking rather than discrete, approach problems and people with a mentality of both/and rather than either/or. Radical feminists often canonize the supposedly feminine side of each of these alternatives. They are slow to admit that stereotypically feminine and masculine ways of thinking and proceeding should have equal rights. If given their preference, radical feminists would have little to do with men and male ways, either taking a respite from the damage that they think male ways tend to produce, or withdrawing permanently, under the conviction that male ways lie beyond redemption.

The majority of women do not subscribe to a radical feminism of this type, but a great many women believe that women do not receive fair treatment in most cultures. The majority of women, in my experience, are feminists, if one means by feminism a desire to see women receive fair treatment. But only a relatively few women think that women's ways of thinking and proceeding are so superior to men's ways that wherever possible we ought to make women's ways prevail and make men's ways cease. Most women accept the two-sexed nature of the human situation as something positive. They may often find themselves hurt by men or frustrated by male ways, but they also admit that having men around brings many positive benefits—not only children, but also ways of looking at the world and expressing the image of God that can lead to wisdom and delight.

### 3. Can a man be a feminist?

It is hard to conceive of a man being a radical feminist, unless he hates his own sexuality. It is easy to conceive of a man being a moderate feminist, someone who perceives many injustices against women and champions women's advance to a full equality with men. Many men are fair-minded, and only fair-mindedness is needed to recognize that many societies discriminate against women both economically and culturally. Certainly, one has to define one's terms. For example, is denying women access to ordination as rabbis, priests, or mullahs (Muslim religious leaders) a form of religious and cultural discrimination? The majority of feminists would answer yes, because they think that women should have access to leadership and power in all social institutions, including religious ones. For men to have such access and women not to have it suggests some inferiority in women—some lack of fittingness in women's mediating between God and human beings.

Obviously, attributing such an inferiority to women is a serious charge, and the societies that have made it have tended to consider women less human than men, because mediating between God and human beings has seemed the high point of our human capacity for wisdom and goodness. Men who agree with feminist women that denying women access to religious authority and leadership is a form of discrimination probably feel similarly about discrimination in business or politics, and so qualify to be considered feminists in a broad, comprehensive way.

Just as whites can oppose racism, and Israeli Jews can champion the rights of Palestinians living in Israel, so men can champion the rights of women and qualify as feminists. In all of these cases, the possibility exists that the apparently stronger party can also suffer discrimination—be treated or thought about unfairly. Blacks can stigmatize whites. Palestinians can hate Israeli Jews indiscriminately. Women can disparage men as a block and refuse to treat Tom, Dick, and Harry as individuals who ought to be judged on their own merits. Nonetheless, the first perception in each of these cases is that the stronger party—the party usually possessing more economic, political, cultural, or even physical might—has to work harder to identify itself with the weaker party and render the weaker party justice, because to do so the stronger party has to give up some of its power, privileges, or sense of superiority. Thus, a man who is a genuine feminist often is quite mature—reflective and goodhearted beyond the normal measure.

### 4. Are feminists lesbians?

No. The majority of moderate feminists are not lesbians. Many radical feminists are lesbians, but by no means all. However, sometimes one encounters a distinction between physical lesbianism and political lesbianism. Physical lesbianism is a biological and social orientation that makes a woman prefer another woman as a sexual lover. Political lesbianism is an identification with other women for the sake of championing women's fight for equality with men in work, education, religion, and the other dimensions of culture. A few women decide to associate nearly exclusively with other women from this political motivation, even though physically they are oriented heterosexually.

The threat of being labeled lesbian is a source of fear, making many straight women slow to call themselves feminists. (Similarly, the threat of being labeled gay can keep heterosexual men from supporting gay rights.) This sad state of affairs shows the merit of charges that many cultures are "homophobic": shaped significantly by a fear of homosexuality, both male and female. A woman does not have to be lesbian to perceive sexism—discrimination and injustice perpetrated along sexual lines (usually against women). One does not have to give lesbian inclinations any favored position to join with feminists in the support of women's wholesale equality with men. One does not even have to approve of lesbianism as a valid moral option, though appreciation of discrimination against women sufficient to make them feminists tends also to make people tolerant of lesbianism—respectful of women's right to choose their own sexual life-styles.

## 5. Why are feminists so angry?

Just as fear of being labeled lesbian makes some women hesitate to call themselves feminists, so does the charge that feminists are angry women, women turned sour on men, women you can never please. This is a calumny. Some feminists are angry, and sometimes their reasons do not seem to support the depth of their anger. But many feminists are not especially angry, and many women who do not call themselves feminists are powerfully unhappy (and so usually angry in their depths). Those who try to manipulate women away from feminism by accusing feminists of an unattractive anger often play on the stereotype of a lady as a woman who never gets angry—who considers anger unrefined, not genteel, something that nice women stay away from. This is highly debatable.

Feminists are properly angered by injustices against women. When they see the statistics on poverty, spouse abuse, rape, and other indices of how people mistreat one another, they note that women often appear to be suffering more than men. For example, many more men batter women than women batter men. The number of women who rape men is miniscule compared to the number of men who rape women. The vast majority of single-parent families are headed by women. The people at the bottom of the totem pole, when it comes to poverty, dependence on welfare, access to jobs that pay well, and the like, are women from minority groups. People who think that women ought to be treated as the equals of men, and that race or ethnic background should not determine one's economic or social opportunities, grow angry at these statistics. People who see women battered and raped rightly take a dim view of the men who perpetrate such violence.

Feminists are also bound to be angry at the injustices found in the historical record. They are bound to think that women's second-rate status in most periods of history is a negative judgment against the human race. Certainly, a few women who call themselves feminists rage beyond what most other feminists consider a proper measure. To simply call men evil and expect no good from any man is to go far beyond what most women have experienced. But it is also unjust, itself a significant evil, to brand feminism a product of women's unbridled, immature or self-serving anger. Feminists are not "so angry" as a matter of course. The degree and justice of their anger varies from person to person, as does that of people who suffer racial, ethnic, or religious discrimination. There are objective reasons for feminist anger, and only those whose minds are closed to the facts about discrimination against women fail to admit them.

### 6. Don't feminists really want to be men?

Though this question arises regularly, sometimes from women, I find it hard to take it seriously. No healthy woman wants to be a man, as no healthy man wants to be a woman. Any healthy woman can see benefits and penalties in being a man, as any healthy man can see benefits and penalties in being a woman. But mental health requires a solid self-acceptance and self-love. We are what we are, and the religious among us accept what we are as the doing, the gift, of God. Not to accept what one is is to kick against the goad and suffer grievous pain. Apparently a few people become convinced that they are imprisoned in the wrong sexual body, but this is rare and pathological. Indeed, the severity of the cure—an operation to change one's sex—suggests how troubled the individual has to be.

The charge that feminists are women wanting to be men draws its slight plausibility from the favored status that men have enjoyed in the great majority of cultures. By and large, boys have looked forward to a future richer in opportunities than have girls. Leadership, wealth, independence, and scope for creativity have all been richer for males than for females. Subordination and second-class status have kept the majority of women from thinking of themselves as independent agents and exercising the full range of their creativity. Recognizing such a state of affairs, many women have wished that they had the opportunities available to their male counterparts.

Seldom, however, has this led such women to a full desire to be men. Not only has realism shouted that one has to accept what one has been made to be, women's privileges have also stepped forward to indicate how female existence can be full of graces. In addition to the miracle of motherhood, there have been women's wisdoms about cooperation and friendship, women's skills at decoration and beautification, and women's ability to pray. Burdened with less social ego, many women have come into their later years remarkably free to love God and enjoy the mysteries of both nature and society. For such women, being female seems an obvious blessing—a wonderful way to have been made. Indeed, the feminism of such women often amounts to an effort to publicize the equality with men that women's ways of being human make obvious.

### 7. How can men and women be equal?

Usually this question assumes that the sexes are very different biologically and psychologically. It then equates difference with inequality, a bad mistake in logic. Women and men are both similar and different. Both sexes can reason and feel. Rationality and emotion work in men and women alike, all stereotypes not withstanding. Women can be either virtuous or vicious, as can men. Women can wield power well or poorly, selfishly or for the common good. The most mature women are wonderfully wise, as are the most mature men. Given equal opportunity, women can be as good doctors or engineers as men, as good artists or business leaders.

The crux of the feminist perception of women's actual, natural equality with men boils down to women's equal share in humanity: reason, creativity, fineness of feeling, wisdom, sanctity and the other measures one might put forward. To be human is not to be male or female. It is not to think like a man or feel with the delicacy of a woman. It is not something determined by sex, though sex colors it through and through. Jesus called women to faith as consistently as he called men. Women were as fit for discipleship, as much candidates for the kingdom, as men. If men got more of the leadership roles in the early Christian community (women got some), we are prudent to attribute that to cultural conditioning, not to anything intrinsic to femaleness or maleness. Leadership in the Christian community depends on such qualities as learning, goodness, and charisms (gifts) bestowed by the Spirit of God. It is nothing tied to a male body or denied to a disciple with a female body. So, women and men can be equal because God has made humanity (the rich flourishing of our kind) the conjoint possession of the two sexes: "Male and female he created them" (Genesis 1:27).

### 8. Are feminists opposed to marriage and childrearing?

No, though many feminists criticize the arrangements worked out in many cultures as unfair to women. If marriage is a free pledging of love, and an entering upon a fully shared, common existence, then feminists can only applaud it as a valid choice that many women are likely to make as they search for their legitimate fulfillment and happiness.

Heterosexual love is one of the primal wonders of creation. Those who experience it understand fully why marriage is natural to the human condition. But this primal wonder carries within it a strong call for justice, fair-dealing, mutual consideration—in a word, equality. In love, the sexes are made tender toward one another, brought to consider one another's well-being at least as important as their own. If a given culture makes marriage an extension of parents' control over their children, or makes it a process through which a woman becomes the chattel of a man, then that culture falsifies the natural intention of heterosexual love. To subordinate a woman to a man so radically that she loses her equal humanity is to denature both marriage and heterosexual love. It is a great crime, of which many cultures have been guilty, and all feminists decry it.

Similarly, all feminists object to arrangements for childrearing that take away women's dignity or force women to sacrifice their fair opportunity to gain self-expression and fulfillment. How a given culture or a given couple structures the rearing of children is a matter admitting considerable freedom, but the crucial judgment, in the eyes of feminists, is whether women and men share this burden and opportunity fairly. If childrearing is only women's work, then children receive a slanted, inadequate formation. If childrearing forces women to forfeit their natural rights to an education or creative work as rich as that available to men, then women are forced to pay a higher price for parenthood than is just. Feminists decry such an injustice. They have no valid complaint against women being involved, even dominant, in childrearing, but they have to lament situations in which women do this under coercion or to the detriment of both themselves and their children.

## 9. Can a feminist like men?

Certainly. Men are facts, part of the reality that women encounter each day. They are "out there," along with trees, children, office buildings, laws, as well as customs that shape how women dress, speak, think about sex. Some men are bright, attractive, kind, helpful. Other men are dull, unattractive, cruel, a burden. Mature women distinguish between men who help and men who make life more difficult than it would be otherwise. Feminists have to aspire to maturity. They have to hope that their advocacy of women's equality with men will serve them as a pathway to wisdom and goodness. This cannot be done if they are blind to the attractiveness or goodness of the men who fall on the side of the angels.

Still, feminism does tend to sharpen women's judgments about men and clarify the criteria of what makes a man mature and desirable as an admirable specimen of humanity. Beyond physical attractiveness, which many women seem to consider less decisive than do many men, feminist women tend to look for intelligence, sensitivity, an appreciation of women's gifts and burdens, a sense of humor and, for religious women, a hunger for God. To meet these and other significant virtues in male form is undoubtedly intriguing for women of all convictions. The attraction between the sexes is more basic than any political posturings. If people are honest, they have to admit that the world is richer for having two different ways of being human. If they are healthy, they delight in this difference and take it to heart.

## 10. Why are feminists so concerned about inclusive language?

Most feminists realize that the way we speak both expresses how we view reality and shapes our interactions with reality, including the reality of other human beings. If we speak of human nature as male, making "he" stand generic duty for any human being, or using "men" to stand for all human beings, females as well as male, then we establish and reinforce a perception that male humanity is the primary instance of being human, while female humanity is only a secondary instance. In that case, maleness becomes normal and femaleness becomes somewhat abnormal—derivative or even defective. So, for example, the influential classical Greek philosopher Aristotle thought that females were misbegotten males.

The more accurately we can name realities though precise language, the more likely we are to move well through the natural and social worlds. In pressing for linguistic forms that grant women a humanity as primary and significant as that which we grant to men, feminists are only being logical. Since they are convinced that women are as fully human as men, and that this equal humanity has to be honored if both women and men are to flourish fully, feminists are bound to want language to give the full, equal humanity of women its due. Because they find the equal humanity of women to be a matter of extreme importance, they are willing to tolerate the relatively minor inconveniences or changes in style that bringing everyday linguistic usage into line can necessitate. For them alternating "she" with "he" or, perhaps even better, preferring the plural, is a small price to pay for bringing home, day after day, the patent truth that women are an equal half of the human race. It is also a small price to pay for rectifying the longstanding neglect of women's equality that has warped the majority of cultures. Nothing is more central to culture than language. Thus, inclusive language is a central article in the feminist program to heal cultures sickened by sexism.

## 11.  Why are so many feminists unfeminine?

Clearly, this is a loaded question, with many hidden assumptions about what being "feminine" entails. If one takes a definition of femininity that includes the possibility of anger, irreverence, and energetic work to overcome discrimination against women, few feminists need be considered unfeminine.

Many people, both women and men, do not like stridency,

aggressiveness, or even determination, especially in women. They apparently assume that such traits are ill-mannered. One can concede some of their judgment. Gentleness, quiet, and agreeableness can be attractive in either sex, but these characteristics become vices if they block the way to truth and justice. Women who so fear being considered loud or aggressive that they will not raise their voices against injustice are not being feminine. They are being cowardly. It is no part of being a healthy woman to be a coward. People who would pressure women to make cowardice and improper self-abnegation part of being a healthy woman are no friends of women. Their opposition to feminism is often solid evidence that feminism is on the right track. With friends who want to co-opt them to the side of injustice, healthy women need no more enemies! In the final analysis, each woman has to decide for herself what being feminine entails, just as each man has to decide for himself what being masculine entails. I believe that both decisions misfire if they do not make loving the truth and acting on it central.

### 12. What do feminists mean by "patriarchy"?

They mean the rule of society by men, which usually means the subordination of women—to women's being considered inferior, a secondary form of human nature. Historically, most societies have been patriarchies. In most of the societies we know about, fathers have had more say than mothers, official political leaders have been men rather than women, men have predominated in religious rituals and authority. Typically, a female in a patriarchal society is always under the control of a male. A girl requires her father's permission for the key decisions in her life, especially marriage. When married, a woman owes obedience to her husband, who may well control any wealth she has inherited. When widowed, a woman in a patriarchal society may well come under the authority of her eldest son.

Behind this typical state of affairs is a perception, developed and maintained by male cultural authorities, that women are dangerous when left on their own. Stereotypically, a woman alone is flighty, capricious, overly emotional, insufficiently rational, and seductive to men. She cannot be trusted to live peacefully and not make trouble. Thus, male cultural authorities tend to move might and main to tie her down. They tend to write laws and enforce customs that bind women to the senior men in their families. They tend to push women to the margins, making them responsible only for the care of children and the home. In patriarchal societies, men tend to arrogate public affairs—politics, lucrative businesses, higher education, religious authority—to themselves. Sometimes women of exceptional talent or forceful personality can break through such a pattern, but such women will always be rare. Thus, feminists criticize patriarchy as a great foe of women's freedom and flourishing. Only when women are considered the full equals of men (which patriarchy by definition denies) will feminists think that a healthy state of affairs has arrived.

### 13. Is there a standard feminist view of religion?

No, but the majority of feminists view religious institutions as enemies of women's liberation to full equality with men. Some feminists take this position admitting that religion itself moves beyond anything determined by sex to focus on a person's dealings with ultimate reality—the holiness we call God. For such feminists religious institutions that discriminate against women are irreligious, sinning against the best intuitions that experience of the divine mystery raises up. Such intuitions include the sense that people ought to be judged by their goodness and intelligence, not their age, sex, or color. Thus religious institutions that close ordination to women, or will not admit women to higher studies, or say that women have to be reborn as men before they can gain salvation are open to the charge of being bogus interpreters of the divine will.

Feminists who have little religious experience tend to stay on the surface of cultural criticism and reason that institutions that subordinate women to men are plainly women's enemies, pure and simple. If such feminists find that, historically, a given religious institution has burned more women than men as witches, or that it has depicted female nature as the enemy of men's holiness, or that it has wanted men to control women's sexuality, they think that they have valid grounds for labeling such a religion misogynistic—hateful toward women. Thus it behooves religious institutions to prove, by their practice even more than their doctrine, that they are the friends of women's aspirations toward dignity, fulfillment, and equality of opportunity with men. In a word, it behooves them to prove that they love female humanity and see it as a lovely work of God.

### 14. Is there a standard feminist view of work?

No, but the majority of feminists probably incline toward a view that stresses women's freedom to determine their own destinies. For example, all feminists think that women who enter the job market should receive compensation equal to that offered their male counterparts. Further, feminists think that whether a woman works in or out of the home, she should express not simply her husband's desires or the mores of her culture, but even more so her own wishes. In addition, if women have to work outside the home, or even if they choose to work there largely for their own fulfillment, they should not also have to bear the full burden of housework and childrearing. For feminists, both outside work and domestic arrangements ought to reflect women's equality with men. For either work outside the home or work in the home to crush women while men live at ease strikes feminists as deeply wrong.

Work is both a means to support oneself and a means to express oneself. The majority of adult women in the United States now work outside the home, more often than not from economic necessity. If they are to provide for their children, especially their children's higher education, women have to earn money. Many women also want to work. Many find in work outside the home a sense of fulfillment, an opportunity to make a contribution to the common good, without which they would feel diminished, shrunken, ashamed because they had never realized their full potential.

Feminists think that no field of work should automatically be closed to women, and that no field of work should become a female ghetto. Women should have access to the prestigious areas of business, medicine, politics, education, religion, the arts, the sciences, and all other major fields of endeavor. Women should not be conscripted into domestic work or secretarial pools where they are treated as peons. Work is a primary part of being human. Freud defined psychological health as the ability to work (creatively) and to love. Feminists think that women deserve the same rights as men in the matter of work, the same chance at full mental health.

### 15. Why do feminists support abortion?

Not all feminists do support abortion, though probably a majority would describe themselves as pro-choice. Abortion is not an attractive procedure. Those who advocate a woman's right to choose whether she carries a fetus to term usually want to champion the woman's competency to decide what is best, for both herself and the child, and to question whether anyone other than the prospective mother can be so competent.

Certainly, this position, as stated, overlooks the powerful argument that the fetus is personal and has important rights, primary among them the right to live. Religious people who find God involved in conception and consider the prenatal child possessed of a soul making it an image of God have to balk at any untrammeled right to abortion. Some of such religious people are feminists, wanting females to have the same basic rights as men at all stages of the life cycle. Many of them will see a great irony in advocating a woman's right to abort a fetus at will because they know that in traditional cultures female children are less desired than male (and so more often are abandoned at birth). Relatedly, as medical science makes greater progress in determining the sex of fetuses, we witness a greater percentage of female fetuses being aborted than male.

This is only one of numerous ways in which the matter of abortion is shot through with ironies and tragedies. Another is the coexistence of women wanting to adopt children with women wanting to abort unwanted fetuses. Why is it so difficult to match these women? Still a third irony is the coexistence of a strong opposition to abortion with a nearly equally strong opposition to contraception and sex education. Seeing such ironies, many feminists conclude that any people who are not pro-choice are benighted. This is a large mistake, both logically and ethically. It is not difficult to work out a sophisticated position that distinguishes women's proper autonomy from limits imposed by the personal dignity of the fetus. It is not difficult to distinguish abortion from contraception and sex education. It is not even difficult to distinguish various methods of contraception and abortion, as well as to distinguish various reasons for abortion (for example, conception through incest or rape in contrast to conception through sexual license). So while the majority of feminists probably espouse a pro-choice position, one can be a thoroughgoing feminist and oppose abortion as usually immoral.

### 16. Why is it important to fight injustices against women?

Here we come to the moral imperative of feminism. It is important to fight injustice against any group, injustice of any kind. Racial, religious, and economic injustice are the enemies of all people of good will. So is sexual injustice. To carry prejudices and enact discriminations against people because of their sex is contrary to what moral health, a good conscience, requires. It is a sin against the light, and so an offense against God, who is light and no darkness at all (I John 1:5).

Feminism is the obvious, requisite response to the perception that women are being treated unjustly, being discriminated against, because of their sex. Not to be a feminist in the sense of one who opposes such discrimination is to be morally insensitive, dull or even warped in conscience. Various secondary associations of the term "feminism" may put people off legitimately. This primary significance of the term makes a claim on anyone wanting to avoid bigotry, for to discriminate against a person because of her or his sex is simple bigotry. Such discrimination clings irrationally to the proposition that a given sex is inferior, sweeping all individual members of that sex into its warped claim.

Thus, subjectively it is important to fight injustice against women because not to do so is to mark oneself as morally defective. More objectively, it is important because such injustice scars the lives of hundreds of millions of human beings, causing great suffering. Women are the majority of the poor, those abused physically, the illiterate, those kept on the margins of culture. Women are the

great neglected resource, without whose full participation the main-
streams of many cultures limp along. Every blow against injustice
toward women is a blow for the relief of suffering and the welfare of
the human race as a whole. Granted the centrality of women to the
human race, both demographically and psychologically, fighting sexual injustice is a major, some would say *the* major, moral combat of
our time.

### 17.  What do feminists think about the men's movement?

Naturally, opinions vary. My impression, though, is that many
feminists are cautiously for it. On the one hand, the men's movement stimulated by authors such as Robert Bly seems parasitic—a
creature living off the pioneer work done by the movement for civil
rights, the women's movement, and the movements of gays and
lesbians. On the other hand, inasmuch as the men's movement
helps men understand themselves better and gain a better emotional
balance, it deserves the applause of fairminded, charitable people.

Most feminists wish men well. In part, this is a sentiment fueled
by self-interest. A great deal of women's suffering comes from men
who are unhappy with themselves, unbalanced, angry. Any movement that reduces this unhappiness siphons off this anger, and is
likely to lessen women's suffering. Further, feminists who wish men
well are exercising their own better selves. Love, which St. Thomas
Aquinas sometimes describes as wishing the good of the other person, is the habit that most perfects any of us. For Christians, the
more loving we are, the better we express the life of the God within
us. So a disinterested, positive hope for the men's movement can
mark a feminist as charitable and mature.

This said, it remains to add that some characteristics of the
men's movement indebted to Bly and his like disturb feminists.
Sometimes this movement speaks to men as though they existed
apart from women or ought to flee the influence of women like a
disease. That is both impossible and unhealthy. It is impossible,
because virtually all males grow up greatly influenced by their
mothers, sisters, aunts, and female friends. It is unhealthy because
humankind is radically two-sexed. One of the most basic tasks laid

on all human beings is to understand others, and there is no other more basic than the person of the opposite sex. That person forces us to see that being human admits a wide range of interpretations and enactments. Not to accept this wide range, not to love the diversity of the ways in which people can be creative, wise, and good, is to condemn oneself to narcissism, narrowness, and sterility. It is fine for men to traipse off to the woods to beat their drums, stir up ancient images of warriorhood, lament broken relations with their fathers, and experience close, brotherly bonds with other men. It is dysfunctional and bodes ill for both men and women for such men not to return from the woods better lovers of female human nature.

### 18. Do feminists think that women should enter military combat?

This is another matter on which opinions divide. Probably a majority of feminists think that military women themselves should make this decision. Granted that a woman has chosen a career in the military, she ought to have the right to advance in that career parallel to the ways that a man can advance. The word "parallel" here is ambiguous, deliberately so. I don't feel competent to say where the training and assignments of military women ought to be identical with those given military men and where they ought to differ. What seems to me clearer is that the military organizations fail badly if their training, employment, or social understanding discriminates against women or treats women as sex objects. I can imagine circumstances in which a woman's competence as a pilot or even a foot soldier would make her participation in direct combat sensible. If competent women themselves wanted the opportunity to fight in direct combat, I would allow it.

A further question is whether women have any special obligation to oppose both war (the resort to violence as a dramatic means of settling conflicts) and what one might call a military mentality. My impression is that most feminists deny this special obligation, even though they acknowledge that women seem to recoil from violence and conflict more predictably than men. Inasmuch as war signifies a failure of imagination and goodness all around, men have as much obligation to destroy the conditions that spawn war as do women. Inasmuch as violence and conflict are unproductive, dysfunctional ways of settling disagreements, men should try to short-circuit them and find better alternatives just as much as women should. Whether the hormonal differences between women and men, and their different traditional upbringings, allow for such an equal shouldering of the burden to avoid warfare is unclear. Perhaps future studies will give us greater clarity. Still, granted the present inclination of many men in many cultures to bristle at opposition and run quickly to take up arms of different sorts, I am grateful that the majority of women, both feminists and nonfeminists, abhor violence and look for less destructive alternatives.

### 19. What do feminists really want?

More often than not this question comes as a jibe, sometimes a jibe deliberately playing off Freud's supposed puzzle at what women really want. I believe that in both cases the question is nearly impossible to answer, because what women or feminists really want naturally depends on the circumstances in which they find themselves. Speaking generally, one can say that women want justice, freedom from discrimination on the basis of their sex, fair dealing, as well as appreciation, kindness, love, and the other nice responses one can imagine. But none of these desires is peculiar to either feminists or women at large. Men and children of either sex want them just as much as women and feminists do.

Feminists tend to sharpen these desires, however, by focusing on how many of women's frustrations exist because of the cultural limitations traditionally placed on their sex. If patriarchal cultures have tended to restrict women's educational opportunities, as well as women's chances for political power, economic flourishing, and religious authority, then feminists acutely want the demise of patriarchal cultures. In the place of patriarchal cultures, feminists desire cultures that would be egalitarian, granting women opportunities equal to those granted men. Precisely what these opportunities would be, exactly how they would work out in specific geographic areas or social strata, cannot be determined ahead of time. Women and men would have to collaborate, both formally and informally, to ensure that boys and girls faced equally open, bright futures. None of this will ever happen, however, until the pillars of patriarchy (the various priorities that men hold over women) come tumbling down.

It is this tumbling down, this demise of patriarchy, for which feminists most long. Few feminists want a matriarchy, or any other form of government in which women keep men subordinate. Equally, few feminists want an ambiguous culture, in which men hold official power but women rule behind the scenes through sexual manipulation. Most of the feminists with whom I deal want a clean, honest, straightforward acknowledgment of the sexes' thorough equality and mutual need. When feminists feel that they are treated on the basis of their personal talents and goodness, rather than on the basis of their sex, they have the experiential basis for elaborating what they want more expansively, across the board.

## 20. What gains have feminists won?

It is easier to say what gains (American) women have won than to specify which of these gains came from the labors of feminists. On the whole, however, the gains that come to my mind owe a great deal to writers such as Simone de Beauvoir and Betty Friedan, and to organizations such as the National Organization of Women and Planned Parenthood.

Feminists (suffragettes) clearly spearheaded women's gaining the vote. Pioneers in health care such as Margaret Sanger clearly spearheaded women's gaining greater control over their own fertility. Many other women have contributed to women's gaining greater access to such fields of endeavor as medicine, corporate business, laboratory science, publishing, the arts, and theology. Everywhere, women have made great strides in the past two generations. From labor unions to higher education, we now witness a broader representation of women, a greater say granted to women, than was true at the mid-twentieth century. The same holds for politics, religious education, even the military.

This is not to say that any of these dimensions of American culture has become fully egalitarian, even a moderate feminist's paradise. It is not to deny the predominance of women on the welfare roles, the "feminization" of poverty that one finds in both the United States and the global economy. The sorry statistics on the murder of women, the physical and psychological abuse of women, and women's underrepresentation in key aspects of culture continue to mock any claim or assumption that women have gained parity with men.

On the other hand, in the past fifteen years the "female dollar" (what the average woman makes, compared to the average man) has risen from perhaps 59 cents to 72 cents—a significant gain. Even though there is evidence of a ceiling on women's prospects for advancement in many corporations, we now have more women filling upper positions in management than was true as recently as ten years ago. Even the storms over lingering sexism in such areas as medical education (the tempest at Stanford Medical School in 1991 is a good example), are signs that women are getting better at publicizing their grievances, gaining clout and bringing about change. It is hard to imagine any of this having happened had women relied on the enlightenment or good will of men. Each painful incident, such as the Navy's Tailhook Scandal or the televised degradation of Anita Hill, shouts that only a feminist pressure to keep rooting out sexual discrimination will assure that women keep making strides, keep enjoying significant gains toward their rightful equality.

*Part II:*

---

# GOD AND RELIGION

## 21. Does Christianity have a position on feminism?

No. Many different voices clamor to be heard. Scripture guarantees the fundamental goodness of female human nature, by having God make humanity male and female (Genesis 1:27). St. Paul advances this notion by saying that in Christ there is neither male nor female (Galatians 3:18). Admirable biblical women such as Ruth and Esther, Mary the mother of Jesus and Mary Magdalene, show that females can be as holy as males. Yet scripture also shows a bias against women, making wanton Israel a whore like Gomer, the wife of the prophet Hosea, and sometimes using Jezebel, the pagan wife of king Ahab, as a figure for seductive wiles considered innate in female nature. Jesus is even-handed, welcoming women into his community as readily as men, but some scriptural writings attributed to Peter and Paul deprecate women (for example, 1 Peter 3:7 and Ephesians 5:22–24).

Church history manifests the same ambiguity as scripture, no doubt because patriarchal cultures prevailed in both scriptural times and later periods. One can find passages in church fathers such as Tertullian, Chrysostom, Jerome, and Augustine that seem plainly misogynistic. The monastic literature generated in both the east and the west often assumes that woman is a major obstacle to man's spiritual progress. Medieval culture subjugated women to men, and while the Protestant Reformation sought to dignify lay life, it did little to make women the equals of men in either religious or civil rights. Some modern feminists have drawn on religious ideals, but pioneer American feminists such as Elizabeth Cady Stanton found it necessary to edit the Bible, because in their day the going interpretations greatly hindered women's efforts to attain the vote and recognition as the equals of men.

Fundamentalist Christians tend to cling to the letter of biblical texts that subordinate women to men and so to oppose feminists' aspirations to equality. Liberation theologians tend to look on women as one of several large groups held in thrall to social (structural) sin and so especially fit for the relief, the freeing release, that the gospel carries. Thus, Christian faith alone seldom makes people feminists. Nonetheless, feminists seeking a profound rationale for their championing of women's equality with men can find in Christian faith many helps.

For example, Christian faith pictures the destiny of human beings as the gaining of divine life. The grace of God that comes from accepting Jesus as the central revelation of God makes people intimate with divinity during their earthly lives and it flowers in the "glory" of enjoying the vision of God eternally after death. Nothing in this destiny is determined by a person's sex. Women are as fit for it as men. Relatedly, women can be as holy as men, filling the rolls of the saints. For another example, the recent developments in Catholic social teaching spotlight a preferential option for the poor. Since the majority of the poor are women and children for whom women have the primary responsibility, recent Catholic social teaching can place justice toward women at the front and center of faith.

On what many feminists consider the negative side, the Catholic and Orthodox churches, along with many fundamentalist Protestant groups, refuse to admit women to priestly orders or ministerial equality with men. They also are loath to grant women full independence concerning fertility, and often their policies about birth control and divorce work greater hardships on women than on men. Powerful voices from this camp speak of women as the complements of men, rather than as the strict equals of men in all matters of cultural opportunity.

Feminists aware of the repressive dimensions of church history (for instance, violence against women thought to be witches) tend to hear such voices as desiring to continue the subjugation of women to men. Thus, such feminists tend to account Christianity more the enemy of women's liberation than its ally. Only if Christians can show that their Lord and their faith offer women the most profound fulfillment available in current history, and that this fulfillment can pervade all aspects of human existence, can Christians counter this negative tendency and exhibit a credible Christian feminism.

## 22. Is God feminine?

God is as much feminine as masculine. On the one hand, theologians often say that there is no sex in God. As purely spiritual, not limited by a body, God is not sexual—does not speak with a voice of either male or female timbre, does not create by either male fertilization or female conception. If we choose to imagine God in material terms (something that Judaism and Islam forbid), we ought to say that God is neither patriarchal nor matriarchal.

One way to say this is to vary our images of God, so that they all emerge as limited, provisional, more unlike than like what divinity is "in itself." Thus the Bible varies its general depiction of the Lord as male by speaking occasionally of God's feminine aspects. So the prophet Isaiah (49:15) likens God to a nursing mother that can never forget her suckling infant, while the prophet Jeremiah (31:20) speaks of God being moved to the womb in compassion for Israel. The Fatherhood that Jesus attributes to God lays a heavily masculine accent on the entire theology of the New Testament, but the associations that the New Testament makes between Jesus and Wisdom lighten this heavy masculinity, because the Hebrew Bible, on which the New Testament writers depend, tends to personify wisdom as a gracious female.

Christian piety took up this theme of gracious femininity during the medieval period, when many monastic writers depicted Jesus as maternal. Perhaps the most striking imagery occurs in the *Showings* of Julian of Norwich, a text of great theological depth. Julian is convinced that God loves us more intimately and intensely than what even the best of our human loves, which she takes to be the love of a mother for her child, can suggest. Jesus, then, is our mother, the mother of our divine life, loving us more tenderly and passionately than we can appreciate.

The lesson latent in this chapter of Christian piety is that Christians are free to use any imagery for God that does not deny the basic patterns of the New Testament or the basic articles of faith. As well, they are required to subordinate all images to the divine mystery, which ensures that God always remains more unlike than like what we say about God. Thus we may legitimately call God Father or Mother, male or female, lover or friend, but only if we keep in mind the limits of such names. They never capture the fullness of God's reality. Always God remains richer, fuller, better.

## 23. Can feminists call God "Father"?

Why not? Women have fathers, and many of them are good men, men from whom women can extrapolate to a strength and kindness in God lovely to contemplate. Even women whose fathers were not good can imagine God treating them as an ideal father would. This is not to say that women, or men, have to think of God exclusively, even primarily, as their Father. They may think of God as their mother, lover, brother Jesus, guiding Spirit, and much more. They may stop their minds and try to deal with God without thought, without images, in the dark nights and clouds of unknowing that mystics describe. Whatever best nourishes their faith should be their preferred diet.

The fatherhood of God is only problematic because of the distortions introduced by patriarchal cultures. Were fatherhood not so frequently synonymous with heavy-handed authority, let alone a dictatorial control of women's lives, there would be nothing objectionable in predicating it of God. Granted the realities of patriarchal history, however, many feminists find it necessary to distance themselves from the fatherhood of God—to free their psyches from a sense of oppression.

Therefore, it behooves Christians to make it plain that the Fatherhood of God, as the entire reality of God, can never be anything oppressive. In any proper understanding of the Christian God, we become free precisely in the measure that we advance in intimacy with God. Nearness to God is the source of our most profound freedom, not of our servitude. And this is no scholastic, linguistic trick. It is something we can experience. The more deeply we abandon ourselves to divine providence, the more deeply we feel ourselves freed of the worries, fears, and inhibitions that keep us in bondage.

As long as we draw breath, we remain vulnerable to such bondage. If nothing else, death threatens our peace of soul, reminding us that soon our existence will cease, very likely painfully. Abandoning our final fate to a God who is deathless, a Jesus whom the Father raised from the dead, is a powerful antidote to this threat. Even though it does not guarantee that no evil will slash our bodies or spirits, it helps us greatly to believe that evil never has the last word. The last word, like the first word, is the yes of a God wholly on our side, wholly determined to consummate his, or her, desire for us and draw us into beatitude. Like the father of the prodigal son (Luke 15:11–32), the God revealed by Jesus cares little about our transgressions. God's great interest is that we live happily in the bosom of our family, in the heaven for which we have been destined. This is not a father we have to fear, a tyrant bent on controlling our every coming and going. This is a parent, fatherly and motherly, who can barely judge us because of the love blinding the divine heart.

### 24. Can feminists accept Jesus?

Yes. In my view, they certainly can. Jesus liked women, considered women such as Mary and Martha his intimate friends. He sought women out, as the incident of the Samaritan woman at the well (John 4) shows. He gave Mary Magdalene the privilege of first heralding his resurrection. Often he set scenes from women's lives parallel with scenes from the lives of men; for example, following the parable of a man seeking out a single lost sheep (Luke 15:3–7) with that of a woman seeking out a single lost coin (Luke 15:8–10). Even if this parallelism is due to the author of Luke rather than Jesus himself, it indicates that the early Christians remembered Jesus as apt to use examples and figures of speech from the realm of women's experience as from that of men.

The main stumbling block that feminists tend to find to accepting Jesus is the claim that he is the unique enfleshment of God. If God has taken flesh in a man, does this not make masculine humanity privileged—closer to God than female humanity? Christian theologians can deny this inference, arguing that the Logos could as well have taken flesh in a woman. Probably the patriarchal culture of Jesus' time and place necessitated that revelation come through a masculine voice. But just as there is no sex in God, so there is no sexual superiority to be deduced from the incarnation's having occurred in a male human body. The divinity of Jesus does not establish that men are more holy than women, nor that authority among the followers of Jesus has to repose in men.

The crux of any person's acceptance or rejection of Jesus, however, goes deeper than these issues. If either men or women find

Jesus possessing unique words of everlasting life (see John 6:68–69), they have an obligation to cling to him as their savior and lord. Salvation—being healed of one's deepest wounds—is more important than any ideology, feminist or male chauvinist. The healing that Christians find in Jesus takes them into the very life of God. In the very life of God, they may hope to find all that defaces or distorts human existence removed, overcome, relegated to a past, imperfect stage of human existence. In the very life of God, women may hope to have their femininity treasured as never before, just as they may hope to find it properly irrelevant.

The life of God is a blazing fire of light and love. Women are as apt candidates for this life as men. Women should find the promise latent in the divinity of Jesus as thrilling as men do. The Jesus confessed by the Christian creed is no chauvinistic champion of male supremacy. He is meek, humble of heart, an iconoclast bent on shattering all the idols that keep people from realizing their truest fulfillment. For those with eyes to see and ears to hear, he is the guarantor of everything best in the program that feminists now labor to bring forth.

### 25. What status can feminists give to Mary?

A very high one. Feminists taken with Mary's "Magnificat" (Luke 1:46–55) tend to see in the mother of Jesus a strong woman continuing the tradition not only of Hannah, on whom the Magnificat draws, but also Sarah, Miriam, Deborah, Judith, Esther, Ruth, and other biblical matriarchs. For Christians, the drama of salvation depends on the cooperation of Mary. God requests Mary's free assent to being the mother of the messiah. Mary does all for Jesus that any mother does for her child. She wonders at the signs that Jesus has a special destiny, and she follows his ministry with mixed feelings. At his death by crucifixion she stands by, surely nearly overcome with grief. Thus, Christian iconography has stressed her sufferings, as well as the joy granted her as the madonna, the serene mother entranced by the divine child.

Any feminists willing to enter into the cultural world of Jesus' time can find solid grounds for honoring Mary. As well, any feminists aware of the later history of Christianity can understand why the Virgin Mary, mother of God, should have gained so prominent a place in popular piety. For both women and men, Mary became a major role model. Women could pray to her thinking she would understand all their family problems. Men could pray to her thinking she had been the best of Jesus' disciples. Mary came to stand for feminine "grace," in both the natural and religious senses of the word. She was imagined to be serene and beautiful, as well as uniquely favored by God. Even if this imagery threatened to swamp the historical realities of her life, it was virtually inevitable. Just as Christians made Jesus into the ideal human being (cast in male form), so they made Mary both the ideal disciple of Jesus and the ideal female human being.

Certainly, feminists run into problems with Mary's being both virgin and mother. Certainly, some aspects of Christian devotion to Mary have been credulous, while many of the revelations that Mary is supposed to have made in modern times (at Lourdes, Fatima, Guadalupe, and several other sites that have become shrines attracting many pilgrims) have carried right-wing political overtones. The cult of the Virgin, therefore, often seems all too human. Still, a properly sophisticated feminism expects this full humanity, and would be surprised to find a cult not mixed with credulity, or even superstition. The fact is that devotion to Mary tells both historians and psychologists a great deal about the place of women in Christian religion. The fact is that much of that devotion has been positive and intriguing—a matter more fascinating to full feminists than repelling.

## 26. What do feminists mean by the Goddess?

Two principal meanings appear. The first is psychological. The Goddess represents the divine aspect of women, or even of human nature at large. When women go into their depths, the fertility, creativity, spirituality, and other great powers or optimal qualities that they find are the "divine" in themselves, the presence of the Goddess. This meaning tends to be as woolly as I have just made it. Whatever is admirable in women is attributed to the Goddess. The Goddess is immanent in women, convertible with their best qualities. The Goddess may also be external—the best qualities of nature. But for the first group of feminist theorists I have in mind, the main accent is interior.

The second group are largely neopagans, intent on divinizing nature. Their orientation is exterior, rather than interior. They see something divine in the turn of the seasons, the constant increase and decrease of life, the beauty of nature, the intricacies of ecological relations. Presiding over these patterns of nature is a beautiful feminine divinity. She is not so much *a* goddess as *the* Goddess—the overall divinity expressed in the processes of life and death. In keeping with what we can infer from the artifacts of Old Europe, this Goddess has long struck pagans as having as much to do with death as with life. The earth is a great tomb as well as the ever-fecund womb. But death is as natural as life. The wise person (the follower of the Goddess) accepts decrease as readily as increase. We human beings are closer to nature than our modern cultures lead us to believe. We shall be happy, peaceful and joyous, in the measure that we stress this closeness to nature. Thus runs the Goddess religion of the second, neopagan feminist group.

Two further comments seem pertinent. First, neither of the views sketched above reaches "divinity" in the sense that the theologians of the great monotheistic religions have had in mind. Their divinity transcends both the human psyche and the natural world, dwelling far apart, in incomprehensible light, as the creator of both human beings and the natural world. Second, both views tend to generate permissive ethical systems, in the sense that both encourage people to act spontaneously upon their sexual desires, give themselves over to the enjoyment of nature and their own psyches, downplay anything felt to be repressive or labeled sinful. On the other hand, both feminist interpretations of the Goddess also encourage genuine love, connectedness, loss of egocentricity, and other potentially good qualities that can foster gentleness and peace. Feminists who reject the Goddess on theological grounds certainly can join hands with the Goddess when it comes to fostering such positive human qualities.

### 27. How should feminists think of sin?

This question is somewhat loaded. As I suggested in answering the previous question, devotees of the Goddess tend to downplay sin, thinking that a doctrine of sin inhibits people. Certainly, many feminists—probably a solid majority—are not devotees of the Goddess. There is no requirement that people wanting to promote the equality of women with men take over a feminine deity (in good part because any genuine deity transcends sexual limitations and so is as relevant to women as to men). But many feminists have been moved by interest in the Goddess, as well as studies of women's religiosity (which often argue that women's sins are different from men's), to rethink the whole matter of sinfulness.

I believe that penetrating feminist analyses of human nature are bound to grapple with what Christianity has called sin, and that it can be illuminating for feminists to consider structural injustices in the light of the Christian doctrine of "original sin." Original sin is only analogous to personal sin, since it is more a state preexisting individual moral choices than something that individuals choose freely. Nonetheless, it offers a stimulating way to think about all that is wrong with human relations structurally—the warped social pattern into which every child is born.

Inasmuch as females are born into patriarchal social patterns, they are twisted out of shape, bent from the cradle, by various forms of sexist injustice. Frequently, the baby girl is not so welcome as the baby boy, nor is she brought up to think as well of herself as are her male siblings. She soon learns that her opportunities are not as rich as the male's, and it is hard for her to resist the example of other females who have concluded that manipulating men is the best way to prosper (in some cases the only way to survive). All of this precedes anything deeply reflective or freely chosen. None of it may be laid to the new female's account, but all of it is wrong, stretching back along a millennial line of human selfishness and cruelty.

In addition to original sin, acute feminist analyses of human behavior will also contend with the wrongdoing that is freely chosen —with "sin" in the sense of evil that an individual might have avoided. Women and men may differ in the ways that they tend to sin personally, but honest members of both sexes who examine their consciences find plenty for which they have to ask forgiveness. The stereotype now is that men tend to sin through pride and aggression, women through weakness and timidity. This stereotype has some merit but, in fact, moral matters are considerably more complicated. Women who have come into power are not necessarily kinder, gentler, or more just than their male counterparts. Many men are cowardly, refusing to stand up to evil when it might cost them money or status.

Some think that the only way to avoid this entire negative realm of human consciousness is to live superficially, refusing to examine either one's own motivation or that of other people. Because I believe that the unexamined life is not worth living, I am horrified when I hear feminists dismiss the notion of sin and heartened when I find feminists acknowledging that a heightened consciousness makes them more appreciative of human moral complexity and wrongdoing, not less.

## 28. Do feminists make nature divine?

Part of the answer to this question occurs in my answer to question 26, on the Goddess. To fill out what I said there, I need only note that feminists vary considerably in their reaction to theology. First, many feminists think that they have little interest in theology. "Theology" is something that they associate with churches or synagogues, and churches and synagogues strike them as strongholds of antifeminist thinking. Second, many feminists consider themselves secular people, people who find worldly affairs more than enough to negotiate. They are not interested in taking on such issues as God and afterlife, sin and grace. Practically, they are agnostics more than atheists: they do not deny God so much as they prescind from God, say they just don't know about God and, in any case, don't find God relevant to their daily lives.

All of this is bound to sadden the theologian, feminist or non-feminist, because the theologian worth his or her salt thinks that God is the premier reality of human existence and the great beauty. In fact, theologians of my persuasion are bound to think that feminists, like all other human beings, are constantly involved with God, whether they realize it or not. God is the source of the light of their minds, as well as the light of their eyes. God is the end, the term, the fulfillment they are pursuing—the rest for which their restless hearts long. God is love, with a capital "L." God is similarly light, truth, goodness, justice, and all the other positive attributes that good people honor.

However, God is not nature, despite the inclination of Deists to equate God with nature (*Deus sive natura*). For orthodox theologians of all the major monotheisms, God is the creator of nature, the infinite source of all finite existence. All things in nature derive their existence from God, but God is neither identical with any one of them nor their sum. God transcends nature, goes beyond it. God, plus the nature that God has created, is not more than God alone. The beings of nature participate in God, but their participation does not diminish divinity, let alone exhaust it. To say that God is identical with nature is pantheism in a strict sense—God is all, and all is God. This rings in the ears of traditional Jews, Christians, and Muslims as heresy—religious doctrine gone dangerously wrong.

Having said this, I hasten to add that God is present in nature, and that God's presence offers a reason for considering nature holy, something not to be abused at human beings' caprice. There would be no trees, rocks, squirrels, mountains, seas, whales, or zebras without God's grant of existence. Every touch of beauty that one finds in nature points to the beauty of God. The trees blazing in the New England fall tell of the glory of God. So does the delicacy of a baby's fingers, the whorl of its ear. To say that God is not nature is not to say that nature is not a gift of God, a presence of God, a thing we may properly consider holy, sacramental, worthy of reverent attention and use.


### 29. Is sex naturally holy?

This question comes from the desire of some feminists to break away from the fear of sex that has troubled many periods of human history and cast women in the roles of temptresses or beings more animal, and so more impure, than men. To answer it one has to make some distinctions and sharpen the language involved. First, what does the phrase "naturally holy" mean? My theological preference is to think that there is nothing purely natural, in the sense of existing apart from grace, the personal presence of God. Inasmuch as grace makes something holy, one can say that sex or anything else becomes holy in the best sense when it is shaped by the personal presence of God.

However, if one means by "sex," activity that human beings freely choose (rather than the biological division of animals into males or females), one has to propose further distinctions. All human beings may live in a world of grace, where God (for Christians, the Trinity of Father, Son, and Spirit) has made the personal divine life present and active, but many do not think of their lives in this way. For them, sexual activity is as natural as eating and sleeping. They do not see that eating and sleeping admit of influences from God, dimensions of holiness, and similarly they do not see that sexual intercourse carries rumors of angels.

Nonetheless, even more than eating and sleeping, sexual intercourse has the power to reveal the personal presence of the holy God, because on occasion intercourse concentrates the deepest passions of the human being, which flow from love and fear. At its best, human sexuality gives and receives the persons' very selves. Their bodily donation is the medium for giving their souls. At its worst, human sexuality reinforces the fear we all suffer that we are not lovable. Thus, a great deal is at stake in human sexual activity. It is "naturally" holy in the loose sense that many people experience it as tied up with the most thrilling and most painful of their precisely human adventures.

Feminists do us a service when they try to liberate sexual activity from repressive fears. They do women a special service when they oppose the notion that women are less spiritual than men and more tainted by their sexuality than men. But they do us no service when they reduce sexual activity to something commonplace, unlikely to be a revelation of the awesome holiness of God.

### 30. Should there be religious ceremonies for such moments of the female life cycle as puberty, birth, and menopause?

Many religious societies have celebrated such ceremonies. In most of them, women have been thought to carry a sacral power in their bodies—specifically, in their blood. Blood is so closely identified with both life and death that the majority of traditional peoples have surrounded it with taboos. Such taboos have expressed human admiration as well as human fear. If men had the power to kill (in hunting and warfare), women had the complementary power to bring forth life. The power to kill was awesome, and so was the power to bring forth life. The blood associated with women in menstruation and birth therefore became highly charged. Cultures that did their deepest religious business through myths and rituals tended to develop ceremonies to mark girls' coming of age, women's bringing forth new life, and women's passage beyond the time of fertility (into a new time, when greater calm might foster greater wisdom).

Modern cultures, on the whole, are poorer in ritualistic, ceremonial life than older, traditional cultures. Analytical criticism has made it difficult for modern people to enjoy myths and rituals as their ancestors did a thousand years ago. Thus a poverty of imagination and community experience has deprived many people of the sense of meaning that their ancestors enjoyed. Present-day men and women often feel that they do not know what manhood or womanhood entails—a feeling that would have seemed bizarre to their ancient forebears. If new ceremonies would help women and men better understand the tasks laid upon them by their sex, I would be all for them.

For women, coming into adulthood is more than gaining the capacity for physical reproduction, but the advent of this capacity is dramatic enough to make the menarche a good occasion to cele-brate the dawn of maturity. Similarly, the way that we celebrate birth could do much more for women's sense of accomplishment—fulfillment of their biological potential and contribution to the main-tenance of the race. Finally, if ceremonies for menopause stressed women's entry into a rich new phase of the life cycle when they should feel that they have been freed to ponder more deeply the fascinating mysteries of human destiny, we might greatly diminish the sense of rejection that many women experience after age fifty. Inasmuch as many present-day societies evaluate women in terms of their physical beauty, a ceremony for menopause might strike a hearty blow for more significant qualities: intelligence, dedicated service, wisdom, and holiness.

### 31. Why do feminists favor ordaining women?

This question refers to a controversy that has been brewing in many Christian churches (most significantly, the Roman Catholic, Anglican, and Eastern Orthodox) for well over a decade. Feminists usually bring forward two major reasons. First, many competent women feel called to serve as priests. Second, the church as a whole would only profit from the enlargement of its ministerial ranks by such women.

It is true that no one has the right to ordination. Ordination ought to arise from the conjunction of the community's desire that a certain person serve it through sacerdotal leadership and that per-son's willingness, perhaps even eagerness to serve. Nonetheless, the second part of this conjunction is important. If the Spirit of God inspires a given person to desire ordination, and that person has the requisite physical, intellectual, moral, and religious gifts, then the community normally ought to give the person's desire a sympa-thetic, positively prejudicial hearing. Feminists dismiss out of hand the notion that female sex might render a person unfit to represent

God or to minister to the needs of her fellow human beings. Such a negative reading of femaleness is precisely what brings feminism into being: sexist discrimination against women. So feminists argue that a woman desiring ordination deserves the same hearing as a man.

Second, the community is only enriched by the entrance into its ministerial ranks of more competent people desiring to serve their churches. The broader the pool of talent, experience, insight, and gifts of the Spirit, the better the churches are likely to fare. For too long in their history most Christian churches limped along on the talent of only half their members. (The churches that limited ordination to *celibate* males further reduced their pool of talent, to the point where it is possible that they often overlooked the best and the brightest). The results in such areas as the canon law and theology of marriage, the churches' teaching on sex, and pastoral counseling were potentially disastrous. Simple justice to the Christian community as a whole requires both the overthrow of longstanding patriarchal patterns (and the overthrow as well of the self-serving of male powerholders that has keep them refusing to share authority with their sisters) and the admission of women to all ranks of Christian service and authority as the complete equals of men—that is the feminist credo.

### 32. What is feminist Christian liberation theology?

Christian liberation theology makes freeing people who are oppressed the heart of the gospel message. Call such people "the poor," stress how the message and example of Jesus, as well as the power of the Spirit, can liberate the poor from their oppression, and you have a "liberation theology." The best liberation theologies are not simplistic. They realize that "poverty" means much more than low income or few physical possessions. They agree with traditionalists who say that the greatest poverty, the worst oppression, is sin. And they admit that oppression takes sexual, racial, and ethnic lines, as well as lines of class and age. But the heart of the matter remains the address of Jesus' preaching about the kingdom of God to all the poor people suffering from the injustices of the way that "the world" does business.

Feminist liberation theology is that which focuses particularly on the status of women. This liberation theology notes the many abuses on the record of patriarchal cultures, both those that have dominated recorded past history and those still flourishing today. It notes the predominance of women among the economically poor and the politically marginalized. In religious matters, it notes the second-class status that many women have in the power structures of a great many churches, synagogues, mosques, Hindu and Buddhist communities. It underscores the poor image that all the major religious and moral traditions have given women, and women's underrepresentation in the councils of theologians and spiritual masters that have dominated such traditions. In a word, Christian feminist liberation theology wants a reform of both secular and religious culture that takes the message of Jesus to heart and applies it to rid women of the many oppressions beating them down.

### 33. What does feminism say about prayer?

As one might expect, secular feminism says little if anything about prayer. Prayer is a religious activity outside its horizon. Religious feminism may or may not say significant things about prayer. In my opinion, the best religious feminism considers prayer extremely important.

Religious feminists want women to have the same freedom at prayer that men traditionally have enjoyed. Women ought to be able to pray as the Spirit moves them. They ought not to be constrained to patterns that male authors, spiritual directors, or church leaders think ought to obtain in women's prayer. They ought to follow saintly leaders like Teresa of Avila and Thérèse of Lisieux in finding their own pathway.

Women and men both experience God to be the overwhelming mystery of their lives. Both realize at prayer that they are, in Paul's terms, only the pots, never the potter. But they may vary considerably in the images that serve their prayer well. For example, more women than men have found a bridal imagery useful, for obvious reasons. Today more women than men are interested in using the name "Mother" for God. The way that we pray is the most crucial index of our actual religious beliefs. Along with how we treat our neighbors, it is the most crucial way that we fulfill Jesus' twofold commandment. Thus religious feminists should urge women to seize the fullest freedom in their prayer, and to take the greatest responsibility.

### 34. How does scripture depict women?

This is a large question, and the best response might be to refer to the many books that have appeared in the last decade on various aspects of it.

In brief, scripture does not depict women as favorably as feminists would like, yet scripture does safeguard the dignity and holiness of women, as well as indicate from time to time that women can be wiser about the ways of God than men and bolder in carrying them out.

The depiction of Eve sets the tone in much of scripture and displays the patriarchal hands that fashioned the Bible. On the one hand, Eve is the equal of Adam in possessing humanity and reflecting an image of God. On the other hand, Eve is derivative from Adam's rib, his helpmate and delight, and her main initiative is in creating the fall from grace that, mythologically, explains the painfulness of the human condition. She is seduced by the serpent, which allowed many of the church fathers to blame her for original sin.

On the other hand, Mary, the Mother of Jesus, is depicted as the Second Eve, whose free obedience to the desire of God restored the human race to intimacy with its creator. In saying yes to the request of the announcing angel and conceiving Jesus, Mary overcame the fall. With Mary, several of the female disciples stood by Jesus to the very end on Golgotha, when the men had fled. Jesus worked some of his most impressive miracles for women, and every indication is that he found the faith of women at least as impressive as that of men.

One could go into great detail about the portraits of both particular biblical women and female nature in general, ranging through both testaments, but the overall finding would remain ambiguous. On the one hand, scripture represents the patriarchal biases of the cultures in which its human authors lived. On the other hand, the revelatory message of both testaments often breaks through these biases, offering women like Ruth and Mary Magadelene as prisms through which believers may view the amazing grace that the biblical God has consistently offered.

### 35. How do non-Christian religions treat women?

This is another large question, to which I have devoted a book, *Women and World Religions* now in its second edition. The short answer is that all of the non-Christian religions display an ambiguity about female nature at least as acute as that found in Christianity. Judaism displays the ambiguity of the Hebrew Bible, but also that of the rabbinic tradition, which frequently forbade women the right to study Torah and sometimes deprecated female nature as more flighty and sensual than that of men. Islam displays both the subordination of women to men that one finds in the Qur'an and the patriarchal attitudes of the cultures, both Arab and non-Arab, in which the message of the Prophet took hold. Muslim polygamy is perhaps the most potent symbol of women's problems: only men could have a plurality of spouses. Hindu scripture and tradition cast women as less fit for salvation than men, one epitome being the conviction that a woman had to be reborn as a man before she could break the karmic cycle and enter into moksha.

Buddhism gave women more freedom than Hinduism had, but virtually all Buddhist nuns have been subject to male monastic authorities, while seldom has Buddhism directly challenged the prevailing family mores in the cultures that it has converted. Confucian mores greatly subordinated women to men, but Taoist symbols often placed stereotypically feminine traits—indirection, gentleness, apparent submission but actual control through endurance—at the heart of how the Tao, the Way of nature, proceeds. Shinto naturalism located Amaterasu, the sun goddess, at the head of the pantheon, but Shinto ethics did nothing to overturn traditional Japanese patriarchalism.

The record of so-called oral religions (those without writing) is complicated, but on the whole men have held tribal rule while women have enjoyed sacral status as vehicles of life. Most traditional oral peoples have segregated the sexes, in an effort to control both the killing power of men and the generative power of women, and most have also sponsored elaborate ceremonies for both sexes, to dramatize key moments in the life cycle or illumine key tasks. While in oral cultures women might suffer physical subjugation, even physical abuse, they could usually find solid grounds for thinking their contribution to the welfare of their people as significant as that of men.

As a whole, then, the great swath of human history that has unfolded apart from explicitly Christian faith has been neither a paradise for women nor a hell. It has shown many ways in which women have needed the redemption spotlighted in Christ, but also many ways in which what Christians call grace has been at work to cheer women's hearts. Feminists can regard the regular subjugation of women to men in the non-Christian religions as an argument that religion in general has been the enemy of women's equality, but only the ignorant or insensitive among them can fail to appreciate the complexity of women's actual experience with all the religions— the inextricable blending of positive sources of profound meaning and negative sources of suffering.

## 36. Why are women so often considered temptresses?

Patriarchal cultures elaborate their "official" views of the sexes from a male standpoint. From that standpoint, the sexual allure of women can be a potent problem. Whether such allure stems principally from men's desire or women's efforts to be attractive is secondary. The primary consideration is the trouble that the desirability of women causes. This trouble intensifies when men are pursuing a monastic ideal of chastity. Then the sexual allure of women can appear as a leading weapon of Satan. The more passionately monks, whether Buddhist or Christian, seek freedom from all carnal desires, the more diabolical the beauty and allure of women can seem. It is a short step from this notion to branding women temptresses—agents deliberately trying to lead men astray.

The reality naturally is more complex. In cultures where women are not the political equals of men, the temptation is strong for women to gain power through covert means. Since they cannot get a hearing or make a say by honest, straightforward means, women have to find other avenues. If they discover that men desire their beauty, women are tempted to use this discovery to promote their own ends. Not all such ends are wicked or self-serving. Sometimes the bare survival of their children or themselves is at stake. There is little evidence that many women become wicked in this matter, enjoying sending men to their moral doom. There is some evidence that considerable numbers of women take an understandable satisfaction in having found a way to outwit patriarchal biases and ensure their own survival. If the "fight" is not fair, virtually any weapons become legitimate.

This general feminist analysis becomes specific when matters such as prostitution come up for study. Current feminist theory tends to favor an economic explanation of prostitution. Women do not enter so degrading a profession or activity when they have other economic choices. Virtually always they become prostitutes because they see no other way to secure food and shelter. Certainly, a false glamor and seductiveness are essential to the exercise of organized prostitution, but only the youngest prostitutes are likely to be taken in. Selling her body for money repulses the average woman as, indeed, the average man. It is a quick way to develop a profound self-hatred. Analogously, playing the temptress in any serious way repulses the average woman. She longs for a fair playing field and the destruction of all the games of seduction that such fairness might bring in its wake. Apart from the healthy spice of right sexual play, seduction and manipulation are abhorrent to all genuine feminists.

### 37. Can women's weakness be sinful?

This question calls to mind again the distinction some feminist theologians favor between men's tendency to sin through pride or aggression and women's tendency to sin through cowardice—a lack of the courage to be. In this context, women can be sinfully responsible for their collusion in patriarchal patterns of oppression. If they agree to a subordinate role in which they fail to oppose various injustices, including those visited on their own sex, they conspire with forces of darkness, and so sin.

In this connection, the psychoanalytic feminist Dorothy Dinnerstein has coined two memorable images—the mermaid and the minotaur. The minotaur is the stereotypical male, brutally powerful and led dumbly by lust. The mermaid is the stereotypical female, insubstantial and seductive, a singer of siren songs. In Dinnerstein's view, the sexes often collude to keep such stereotypes effective. Men try to dominate by physical force or economic might. Women try to rule by seduction, manipulation, often using sex appeal. Both types of behavior are degrading. Both deny the better impulses of each sex and assure that men and women never enjoy one another as they ought.

The sinful weakness of women can show in their refusal to challenge such stereotypes. It can also show in women's capitulation to low self-images that tell them that trying to live honestly or stand on their own is futile. Here, however, we must be careful, because most of the women who fail to live honestly and stand on their own are battling powerful social forces ranged against them. How culpable a given woman is is usually hard to say. More often than not, even apparently successful women suffer from terrible self-doubt—considerably more than what one finds in their male counterparts. The most obvious source of this self-doubt is the biases of patriarchal cultures against women—the many ways in which they tell women that they are not the equals of men, cannot be competent and strong. The women's movement has made significant progress against this message, but more self-doubt remains than many outside observers suspect. This does not mean that women do not have to examine their consciences, but it does mean that external sinful structures over which women have little control often are playing a powerful role in women's weaknesses.

## 38. Are women more religious than men?

If we judge by cultural stereotypes, which include images of "religion" that stress emotional delicacy, women are more religious than men. They show up more often in church. They seem to have more interest in spirituality, prayer, and religious ceremonies. They display more of such stereotypically religious attitudes as an abhorrence of violence and a tender concern for the suffering.

The problem is that most of these qualities are as much culturally slanted as personally generated. In other cultures, where theo-

logical literacy and extreme austerity have been the hallmarks of
religion, the going judgment has been that men are more naturally
religious than women, that women are naturally carnal and closed
to high religious instincts. In classical Hinduism, for example, men
are considered naturally more passive, cerebral, and serene (high
religious attributes), while women are considered naturally more
active, sexual, and likely to bring about social or even cosmic troubles. Thus women always need the religious control of men because,
on their own, women are extremely dangerous.

The better view, on both Christian and feminist grounds, is that
neither sex has any religious advantage—is "naturally" any closer to
God. God is as much the source and goal of women's religiosity as
that of men. Equally, the holiness of God judges women as severely
as it judges men. Both men and women are free to pursue the light or
hunker in the dark of selfishness. Both are challenged to love beyond
fine feeling, to the point where one does what is right simply because
it is right. Equally, both operate within channels of social conditioning and images telling them what masculinity, femininity, and religiosity ought to mean. Thus each faces the same central task of
human maturation: to gain a proper blend of autonomy from one's
community and also correlation with it.

If men's typical challenge is to bridle their drive for autonomy,
so that they give correlation its due, perhaps women's typical challenge is to bridle correlation (concern for how others think and act)
so that they give autonomy its due. Neither sex can avoid the radical
challenge of Jesus' twofold command. Both have to find proper
ways of loving God wholeheartedly and loving neighbor as self. Inasmuch as this challenge favors neither women nor men, neither sex is
favored as more religious than the other.

### 39. How do feminists regard religious education?

A great many feminists regard traditional religious education as
an obstacle to women's proper autonomy. The traditions that have
pressured women to yield to men, not to speak up in church, to obey
their husbands, and to think of childbearing as their natural vocation and penance have all contributed to women's subjugation and
unhappiness. Certainly, other religious traditions that have spoken

of women's dignity as children of God and their God-given right to self-development could offset these negative influences, but probably the majority of feminists regard traditional religion, including Christianity, as a source of women's oppression.

For example, it is only in modern times that women have been considered fit for higher education and have enjoyed educational opportunities equal to those of men. The typical Christian church long opposed women's higher education, as it long opposed women's gaining the vote. Religious education has often spoken as though women's proper spheres were only the home or the cloister. The wide world of public affairs was the province of men. Only men might plunge into the dirty sphere of business and politics. Part of women's natural task was to redeem men from such dirtiness, by making the home a haven of refinement, purity, and Christian godliness. Sometimes the sexes managed to live gracefully by this view of their religious relations, but often they could bear it only at the price of considerable hypocrisy.

Feminists worth their salt therefore make honesty the first principle of any acceptable education, whether religious or secular. Women have to be free to learn the truth, advance the truth, cut through stereotypes and hypocritical images erected for improper self-advantage. The opponents of truth are legion. They wax fat inside the churches as well as outside. But they stand against the living God, and so any living, genuine religious education has to oppose them. When a religious education oppresses women, as when it supports policies oppressive to people of color, it forfeits its claim on loyalty. To preach the gospel in ways that bind people more than liberate them is to run counter to Christ. Thus, feminist critiques of traditional religious education can greatly abet liberation theologians, alerting them to ways in which the gospel is being preached against the intentions of its Source and Master.

### 40. How important is self-sacrifice?

Here the issue bubbling in the background is the feminist charge that the spirituality traditionally offered to women in many churches has encouraged them to a self-sacrifice neither asked of men nor helpful to women's proper development. I believe that this

charge has merit. In patriarchal churches (the vast majority), men
have depended on the docility of women. They have also urged
women to be self-sacrificing wives and mothers. They have curbed
women's ambition more frequently than that of men. They have
been willing to write off women's desires, talents and hopes more
easily than those of men.

For example, women in religious orders have had less control of
their own affairs than men. They have been subject to male powerholders (bishops, Roman authorities), whereas men have not been
subject to female powerholders. Only recently have religious women
enjoyed either free access to higher education or the major say in the
sort of work they do. Only recently has it become thinkable for
women to develop lives of their own, apart from the patterns sanctioned by patriarchal churches or societies.

Self-sacrifice obviously can be a wonderful expression of love.
Jesus on the cross remains the great symbol of Christian love. But
women should not be held to this standard more than men. Fathers
should sacrifice for their children as much as mothers. Admittedly,
the sacrifice involved in physical birth is closed to men. But millions
of men have sacrificed their lives to hard work on behalf of their
families. Hundreds of thousands have sacrificed their lives in
priestly ministry. Only the conceit that women's lives were worth
less than men's or held less promise than men's could have sup-
ported the traditional tendency to ask women to sacrifice more of
their autonomy than men. Feminists are bound to oppose any lingering presence of this tendency, because they are bound to think
that women's lives are worth just as much as men's.

The answer to the question, then, is that self-sacrifice is very
important, if one follows Christian standards of perfection, but that
self-sacrifice applies no more directly to women than to men. All of
us will be judged by the quality of our love. Each of us will have to let
go of our lives at death and give everything over to God, in trust that
God will receive us mercifully. Women have no less obligation to do
this than men, but also no more. Outsiders make no more claim on
the charity of women than on the charity of men, but also no less.
Finding the balance between love of self and love of neighbor con-
fronts both sexes as a central moral challenge. Proper self-sacrifice is
as beautiful in male garb as in female.

*Part III:*

BETWEEN WOMEN AND MEN

## 41. What is a proper equality in marriage?

Proper equality is one that honors both the generic parity of women with men and the particular endowments of the given spouses. Any marriage that feminists are going to approve operates on the basic principles that women and men are equally human. Further, it depends on an honest recognition of the talents and needs of the given people involved. If Marie is the one more talented with figures, better able to handle money, then Marie should do the accounts and plan the budgets. If Jake is the better cook, it makes sense to have Jake take primary responsibility for the meals, especially those to which guests are to be exposed. The same applies to teaching the kids to drive, dealing with backward coaches, negotiating the mortgage, placating the in-laws. Consistently, the rule ought to be that fairsharing is the bottom line and that recognizing the respective talents of the woman and the man is the obvious part of common sense.

Marriage is a covenant, a mutual commitment to share life as God dispenses it—for better or worse, in sickness and health. Unless there is parity in this relationship, a similar tally on both sides of the equation, marriage fails to be what it promises, what the spouses had in mind when they entered upon it. The full fertility of marriage depends on the complete contribution of both partners. If one is frustrated or repressed, underappreciated or overly burdened, the marriage can only limp along. So while a proper equality has to be determined case by case, as the individual spouses themselves find best, one can say generally that if either spouse feels less than half the team, the marriage is in trouble.

The feminist ideal for marriage, therefore, is that it serve as a miniature of the relations that ought to obtain between men and women across the board. Throughout society, in places of work, schools, churches, hospitals, laboratories, and all the other sites where men and women gather together, the ideal is for people to interact as equals. Each ought to contribute according to his or her talents, to draw from the common pool according to her or his needs. This is a "communist" ideal, in the sense that it assumes that all of us human beings are in "it" (the venture of being human, making a world fit to live in) together.

Christian faith deepens this ideal by asserting that all the "members" of Christ are like branches of a single vine, limbs of a single body. The church is a great, holy organism in which each member is vitally important and ought to be cherished. Thus, for the church to show itself as sexist, racist, insensitive toward the poor, or in any other way less than radically democratic, intrinsically egalitarian, is for it to fail the body of Christ miserably. That is why good marriages challenge the church, as well as the rest of society, urging it to live up to its better nature and really act on the Pauline conviction (Galatians 3:28) that in Christ there is neither male nor female, neither slave nor free.

## 42.  How should women handle succeeding better than men?

Tactfully, and this for two reasons. First, in patriarchal cultures it is bad form for women to succeed better than men. For a woman to earn a higher salary or gain greater social power can seem humiliating to the men around her. This is largely the men's problem, but they are as much victims of patriarchal warpings as women, so prudent women deal with injured male egos delicately, gently, tactfully.

Second, beyond the prudent tactics enjoined by the psychological realities of patriarchal cultures lies the better ideal of simple human kindness. Any astute analysis of human nature, female as well as male, realizes that all human beings are liable to fits of jealousy and insecurity. Thus, no kind person flaunts success, rubs the faces of other people in the rich chocolate of her or his current prosperity. Beyond the magnanimity of not wanting to injure others, a proper humility keeps mature people from boasting or constantly reminding others of their prowess. One ought to be embarrassed by praise, even that which is not fulsome, because one ought to know how much good luck or fortunate personal history contributes to any success one enjoys. There but for the grace of God go I—less well paid, less well educated, less confident and more fearful.

In situations such as marriage, women have to bring all their tact to bear so that their success does not seem to diminish their spouses. To be sure, mature, loving spouses will only rejoice in their success, but the pressures of patriarchal societies are such that the majority of men will have to swallow hard when they see their spouses apparently outstripping them. For a woman to earn more than her husband may be fine when they tally the bank books, but at other times it can run against what a man has been brought up to expect.

To put the best face on such an expectation, we can note that many men have supposed that they would be the primary breadwinners, and that providing handsomely for their wives and families often plays a central role in men's fantasies of success. Much of the chivalry they expected to offer their ladies fair stemmed from their ability to make life comfortable. When their ladies fair turn out to be ladies more proficient, the men have to step back and retool. The best of them do this admirably, and any men who love their actual wives, in contrast to the fantasy figures they refuse to let go of, find it relatively easy to rejoice in their wives' successes. Still, on several grounds, none of them opposed to feminist convictions about women's equality with men, good women carry their success lightly and make tact their middle name.

### 43. Should women take the initiative in sex?

This is completely a matter of the individual woman's inclinations and the relationship she has with a given lover. Socially, most women will have grown up conditioned to be responsive rather than initiating. Certainly, there are sanctioned ways in which women can show their interest in men, are allowed to start a relationship smoldering or throw more branches on the fire. But in the main, the overt patterns continue to be that men propose and women dispose. In the main, things begin to crackle between a man and a woman when a man shows his interest and a woman, flattered, finds that she is similarly interested in him. Desire tends to increase exponentially when we find that people to whom we are attracted find us attractive. We desire them much more than people who seem barely aware of our existence or unmoved by our interest.

Feminists think that the sexes ought to enjoy fully equal liberties. This does not mean that women have to ignore the social patterns that tend to prevail in their cultures, or the Christian restrictions that limit sexual expression to marriage. It simply means that, through the language of a given culture, women ought to receive the same chances for self-expression and fulfillment that men receive. In cultures that do not inhibit women's ability to receive such chances, women ought to be free to invite men out, show emotional interest and physical affection, even suggest sexual relations, when that is fitting.

All this is especially true in marriage. Spouses ought to work out fairly expectable patterns, according to what they know of their own inclinations and regular tendencies, but such patterns ought to be flexible, allowing for exceptions that prove the rule, and they ought to honor the needs and desires of both spouses equally. Thus, if it turns out that Marie likes to get things going now and then, both Jake and she ought to applaud this as a good thing—a fine way to keep their love flourishing.

### 44. How should women react to abuse from men?

Strongly negatively. No person has the right to abuse another, whether physically, verbally, or emotionally. On occasion any of us can lose control and lash out verbally, even at people we love more than life itself. But whenever such lashing out becomes regular, habitual, the relationship has turned sickly and needs to be cured. Usually the best way for women to initiate such a cure is to withdraw. Women do better to leave an abusive situation than to stay in it from fear, guilt, or a false sense of responsibility. Admittedly, the welfare of children can complicate a situation of domestic abuse, but even when children are a factor women are wise to consider withdrawing. It is likely, even probable, that the children also will become objects of abuse, and it is arguable that children are injured psychologically anytime they see their mother or sister being battered.

The difficulty with which many women remove themselves from abusive situations testifies to the lack of confidence, the doubts about their self-worth, that trouble the females in most patriarchal cultures. Having been brought up to think of themselves as second-class citizens, it is easy for women to conclude that they are also second-rate human beings—less valuable or dignified than men, more properly abused. Those who would help women suffering abuse therefore have to work hard to shore up the women's self-confidence and convince them that it is indeed right for them to withdraw from abusive men, that they are indeed correct when they feel that nothing they could do, no failure in their performances as wives and mothers or in their characters as Bessie or Sue, makes it proper for a man to hit them, or curse them, or tell them they are no good. No man has the right to do that to a woman, because no child of God has the right to do that to another child of God. Indeed, Jesus says that anyone who calls another child of God "fool" is liable to hellfire (Matthew 5:22).

### 45. Why do men dislike how women think?

Not all men dislike how women think, and not all women think alike, in stereotypically feminine ways. Some men are charmed by women's penchant for the concrete, by women's intuition, by women's inclination to personalize many equations. Some women are more logical than their average male counterpart, more hard-nosed, more inclined to rigor and a detached impersonalism. Granted all this, however, it remains that men often shake their heads at women's ways of proceeding, as women often shake their heads at men's ways.

For example, the now hoary chestnut is that men will not ask directions, while women can do so easily, with no sense that they are losing face. Men will not ask directions, in many cases, because to do so seems to them to entail losing status. They become subordinate to the person of whom they are asking information, and they do not like to put themselves in such a position. As Deborah Tannen has shown in her interesting book, *You Just Don't Understand,* this is a matter of competition and social grading built into men's speech. Women are used to being considered subordinate, so it bothers them less to ask for help and so seem inferior. Women also are better able than men to be pragmatic about matters such as this, realizing that seeming inferior is a small price to pay for not losing precious time driving in circles.

The main matter at stake in situations of cross-sexual misunderstanding or irritation is dealing with otherness. Men and women always remain somewhat alien to one another. Simply in virtue of having different bodies and social upbringings, the sexes are bound to find one another strange, perhaps even weird on occasion. To negotiate this strangeness and discover a humanity as rich, and in its own ways as rational, as one's own is one of the greatest challenges and delights that human beings can experience. It is the French *différence* that gives savor to heterosexual interactions. So the crucial aspect of this question is moving men from a dislike of women's ways of thinking to an acknowledgment that difference need not mean inferiority. When men can admit that women's ways are merely different from their own, not necessarily worse, they ought to be able to smile more than frown.

### 46. What are feminist models of leadership?

Feminist models of leadership are sketches of how women either typically tend to run affairs or ideally would do so. The main premise that one finds in feminist literature on this matter is that women's ways of leadership are or should be non-hierarchical. Feminists tend to consider "hierarchy"—ranking people as above or below, superior or inferior—an abiding sin of patriarchal institutions. Stereotypically, men want to know where everyone stands in a group, who has what degree of status or power. They also want to ensure that their own power places them near the top. So their inclination is to cast leadership as something flowing from the top down. Initiative and direction ought to come from superiors. Inferiors ought mainly to listen and obey.

Perhaps because they have so long been "inferiors" in most cultural situations, women react negatively to such a hierarchical arrangement. They tend to draw their chairs into a circle, in instinctive recognition of the fact that everyone deserves an equal say. As well, they want everyone to see the person speaking, be able to deal with her face-to-face. They resent communication that is veiled, anonymous, does not give them a chance to weigh expression, gesture, tone of voice, bodily nuance. In addition, feminist theory argues that the best successes come when everyone owns a given effort, when it emerges as a product of the whole group. Any group is impoverished when some members feel that they are inferior, second-class, not likely to have their ideas valued or welcomed.

Christians are bound to link these feminist ideas about leadership with the ministerial notion of authority that Jesus proposed ought to rule in his community. He did not come to be served but to serve (for example, Matthew 20:28). Admittedly, Jesus was the clear leader in his community, but the rest of the flow chart is hard to determine. Peter succeeded to leadership, but what were the relations among Peter, James, John, and then Paul? Eastern Christianity has preferred a collegial model of upper church authority to the monarchical model developed in the west. While there are many problems with the ways that eastern Christianity has handled leadership and power throughout its history, women can still applaud this democratic instinct. The Pauline figure of the body and the Johannine figure of the vine and branches are both organic. Both can be read as stressing the significance of each member of the group, and so as exposing the poisonous effects of models of leadership that become hierarchical to the disheartening of supposedly lower, inferior members. In a word, both are close to feminist instincts about leadership.

### 47. How can women escape the tyranny of physical attractiveness?

Only with much help from their friends, ideally male friends as well as female. A culture such as that of current mainstream America stresses youth and physical attractiveness. Whatever progress women have made toward equality with men, they have yet to crack the hold that the advertising industry has gained over both the male and female psyches on this score. Men are daily bombarded with images of women lithe and beautiful. To a lesser extent, women are bombarded with images of men tall and broadchested. Both sexes are also told that these are the models they ought to match. They are told that they will only be attractive, sexy, significant, winners, if they are slim, young, vigorous, turned out in four-figure outfits.

Women have to be helped to learn to distinguish between the attractiveness that comes from good health, good grooming, intelligence, wit, interest in others, and similar attributes that any of us can aspire to attain, and the attractiveness that is mainly a matter of fortunate genes, youth, and perhaps working out three hours a day with free weights. Psychological studies show that women have worse images of their bodies than men do, no doubt because women's bodies are more prominent in the popular cultural evaluation of female attractiveness than male bodies are in the popular cultural evaluation of male attractiveness. Stereotypically, women are more interested in the whole of a man's being than men are interested in the whole of a woman's being. Women determine more by ear—what a man has to say, how he sounds, whether he is full of himself or good-humored—than men do. Men determine more by eye—how a woman looks, whether she is foxy.

Naturally, mature men and women alike break this stereotype, but the cultural pressures on women to be slim and beautiful run deep. Therefore, whatever helps women to think of their ideal as something more intellectual, cultural, or even religious than merely physical is extremely helpful. Women should want to become fully rounded, good, helpful human beings. They should aspire to an honesty and lovingness that put them on the side of the angels, regardless of their waistlines or hemlines. Women can get much help in this effort from other women, but they also need the help of fathers, brothers, husbands, lovers, and male friends. Whenever a man responds well to a woman because of her brains as well as her looks and dress, he does feminism a good turn.

### 48. Should menopause be a crisis?

No, not in the ordinary sense of the word. Menopause, like menstruation itself, is a completely natural process. It happens to all healthy women. It is part of the normal female life cycle. If on the surface it marks dramatically a woman's passage from the years when she can bear children to the years when she is beyond those wars, its deeper significance remains to be determined. Women suffering the tyrannies of cultures that prize youth (skin without wrinkles) as the prime index of feminine attractiveness are bound to find painful both menopause in particular and aging in general. Women who have defined their goal as a steady increase in wisdom and love are likely to have fewer problems with both menopause in particular and aging in general.

To be sure, menopause has some purely physical features that can be unpleasant regardless of a woman's overall sense of what her life means, where her worth resides. Hot flashes and cognate symptoms never become desirable. On the other hand, many studies of pain, and phenomena such as menopause, underscore the importance of attitude and mental orientation. If women expect menopause to be a crisis, they are likely to find it difficult. If, on the other hand, they approach it as something completely natural, not necessarily more traumatic than men's balding or lessening of sexual drive, they are likely to find it only a nuisance, not a crisis. The many studies of menopause now appearing under feminist banners do their best work by suggesting how this experience can invite women to a new phase of their lives in which they become more reflective, more detached, more concerned with the lessons that aging and death hold out. (The popular books of Germaine Greer and Gail Sheehy, to mention just two authors, are instructive in this regard.)

## 49. Do women and men need different spiritualities?

Yes and no. Feminists have taken over the word "spirituality," detaching it from its religious roots. In mainstream feminist usage, a spirituality is simply an existential pathway—a regime that makes life more meaningful, more fulfilling. Inasmuch as our sex colors all of our lives, a useful spirituality clearly is going to acknowledge our femaleness or maleness, ideally coming to grips with the challenges we face specifically as women or men. For women, a natural challenge such as menopause is fair game, even requisite game, for their spirituality. For men, the physical liabilities in "type A" behavior (drivenness) is similar. One could say much the same about women's problems with cultural ideals of physical beauty, with men's problems with cultural ideals of autonomy or hardnosed leadership. Any viable spirituality has to meet the actual needs of the people it would direct. Therefore, men and women need somewhat different spiritualities. This applies fully to spiritualities based on religious convictions, leading to the conclusion that women can profit from treatments of prayer, spiritual direction, religious education, work, sexual activity, and the like that take into account concerns specific to them as women.

On the other hand, any spirituality that deals with our most profound problems—suffering, death, injustice, creativity, searching for God, fostering love—ventures upon experiences and intellectual dilemmas that are simply human: shared by men and women equally. Both men and women suffer. Both can experience the ecstasies of creative work, or mystical prayer, or romantic love. Both need wisdom, and fortitude, and temperance. Both need faith and hope. Thus the best spiritualities combine perennial human issues with issues topically particular to women or men. The best spiritualities follow a pattern of both/and, rather than a pattern of being either simply for women or simply for men.

## 50. Is it harder for women to tell the truth than men?

In some ways, yes. Although women are made for the light as much as men, the social formation that women receive in patriarchal cultures tends to give them a different sense of the light than that given to men. Thus, men can find women less direct than they would like, more evasive. In some cases this is simply men's bias, their wanting women to be exactly like themselves (which to women can sometimes seem brutal). In other cases it reflects fears that women have to deal with, many of them fears of offending men who can do them harm.

For the majority of women, truth does not exist in a vacuum. It is not something one can extract from feelings and relationships. What telling the truth will do to the person who receives it is nearly as important as expressing the truth itself. Thus women can be overly sensitive to the impact of their message. They can be strongly tempted to water down bad news. The best way for them to avoid this temptation is to consider what happens when language becomes devalued—when their words lose credibility.

If every child in a classroom hears only praise, then neither Tommy nor Sally is going to think much of being praised. If all evaluations of people's work are positive, then no worker is going to be elated at receiving high marks. Our words, our judgments, have to be realistic. They have to be credible as serious grapplings with a complex world that usually is a mixture of good and bad, high performances and low. The best thing that women can do for others, whether their children, their spouses, or their friends, is to render the complexity of reality as faithfully as they can—but never without gentleness and sympathy.

When there is bad news to tell, women have to be able to tell it, even as they try to soften its blow by standing with the person who must receive it—by extending their emotional support. They cannot let their awareness of the fragility of male egos or females' need for support cause them to denature the truth. They have to honor the light, even as they honor their bonds of common humanity with the person whom the light may wound and display their sharp awareness of all people's vulnerability.

### 51. Are women naturally manipulative?

This charge clangs in a feminist's ear. First, there are many manipulative men. Second, manipulativeness is a stock part of the negative stereotypes of women, something nearly as hard to deal with as the question, "When did you stop beating your wife?" Third, the plausibility in the charge comes from the social pressures laid on women in patriarchal societies, where they are brought up to please men.

What is manipulation? It is moving someone by hand, as though he or she were a puppet. Do some women become skillful at this? Yes, as do some men. Manipulation carries the further overtones of dishonesty, duplicity. People are led to expect one thing, to think that the manipulator is moving them in one direction, with their consent and for their good, while all the while the manipulator is actually moving them in another direction, without their awareness and for the manipulator's own good. Thus, the connotations of "manipulation" are overwhelmingly negative.

In the measure that we love the light, want dealings to be straightforward, we are bound to hate manipulation. (It follows further that honest women are bound to hate having their sex stereotyped as manipulative.) Thus it is extremely important that all friends of women fight the social conditioning that women receive in patriarchal societies and make it easier for women to do business in the light. It is also extremely important that both women and men point out the many ways in which male powerholders shade the truth, connive and deal duplicitously.

There is nothing natural in either sex's becoming manipulative. In either case it is a failure to attain authenticity, a sin against good conscience. Feminists also have to make the case that the special pressures on women to become manipulative—fear of offending men, fear of physical abuse by people stronger than they, desire not to hurt others by a harsh rendition of the truth—should be discussed fully and reduced markedly.

## 52. Why do women share more easily than men?

If this assumption is true, probably it applies best to emotional sharing—being willing to express how one feels, what one is going through. The stereotype in this matter is that men do not share their emotions easily. Their bonding seldom includes explicit discussion of how they feel, what they are going through internally. In contrast, women grow up talking about boys, about other girls with whom they cannot get along, about their husbands, their kids, the people with whom they work. The popular conception, therefore, is that female friends tend to hold one another at ransom, deliberately and gladly, through sharing fairly intimate matters. It is hard to say how fully this conception holds up, because a counter-conception has it that women trust one another less than men trust their fellow men.

Sharing implies a relational image of existence, selfhood, and happiness. On the whole, women treasure autonomy less than men. They tend to clarify how they think and feel by talking about it.

They need others, a circle of friends and collaborators, to feel secure about making their way. In some cases this reflects women's lack of self-confidence. They establish mutual dependencies, and mutual revelations, to shore up egos that might not be able to stand alone. In other cases the relational character of women's social orientation is more straightforward and reflects considerable common sense: this is simply a good way to get things done. Finally, people interested in other people, fascinated by the human comedy, watch and probe naturally, give and take for the fun of it.

If a given woman is insecure, prone to relate to others in significant measure because she fears standing alone, then the next phase of her maturation calls for a dose of independence, an increase in autonomy. Many feminists have organized for such autonomy through the women's movement, inasmuch as they have seen freedom from the control of men as a good thing. Correlatively, men who stand well alone but have difficulty connecting with other people ought to see the next phase of their maturation as a challenge to relate better to others—to share more generously, conceive reality more socially. For both sexes, the ideal ought to be the ability to be both independent and related. The richest humanity is that which can enjoy both solitude and conviviality, that which is both a full self and a glad member of a community.

## 53. How should women regard autonomy?

As the prior answer suggests, autonomy can be the next step in an overly dependent, insecure woman's march toward maturity. It can also be a man's bugaboo, keeping him from a properly rich social life. Autonomy need not mean isolation. It ought to mean simply the capacity to rule oneself well. The opposite of autonomy is heteronomy—taking one's directions from outside, not being master of one's own soul. Religious people tend to say that the fulfillment of autonomy comes with theonomy: joining one's will, one's self, to the reign of God.

If we examine what Jesus meant by "the reign of God," we find that it is a prime example of theonomy. By the grace of God, we can become what, on our own, we can only glimpse. The peace and joy for which we long, the love of others and fulfillment in community, are hallmarks of the reign of God. They come into being when people become passionate believers—disciples who have entrusted their fate to Jesus completely.

Jesus could not work miracles until people gave him their faith. As long as their hearts stayed closed, he could not move through their spirits to heal their withered limbs, staunch their fluxes of blood, open their blinded eyes. So when it encounters the grace of God, a proper autonomy has to expand, yield any suggestion of self-sufficiency. Freely, God offers us the chance to become more than what we can be on our own. In accepting this offer, we have to confess the plain truth of our sins and inadequacies—all the ways in which we have shown ourselves unable to be either our own redeemers or adequate lovers of our neighbors.

I believe that all this means that feminists have to think about autonomy with a proper sophistication. On the one hand, they have to applaud the movement of women who have lived heteronomously, by the will of something outside themselves, into autonomy, a mature self-determination. On the other hand, feminists ought to acknowledge the wisdom of the religious traditions and see that none of us can be our own saviors. Our hearts are restless until they rest in a God who transcends us and is not subject to our control. Our evil is more than what we can expunge on our own: we need the illumination and forgiveness of a divine Lady or Lord. To combine both hands, perhaps so that they join in prayer, requires an unusual sophistication, but one that I would have all feminists target.

## 54. How should men regard relationships?

The answer to this question is also latent in the answer to question 57, but elaborating upon it seems worthwhile. Men ought to regard relationships as part of mature human existence. They ought to criticize as immature, the product of male fantasy, images that idealize the lone ranger, the solitary hero who needs no one, is complete in himself. No human being is complete in himself or herself. All of us need other people, and all of us need God. Divinity itself is not solitary. If the Christian image of the Trinity conveys anything, it is that God is innately social. Father, Son, and Spirit are constituted by their relationships. They are personal (though only analogously to the way that we human beings are personal, because they are not limited centers of consciousness) because their awareness and love shape them mutually. For example, the Father is the Father because and as he generates the Son.

Relationships are more than one-to-one connections and dealings. As they both go in several directions and converge at many points, relationships weave our communities. Our communities, from the nuclear family to the local church, are the places in which we become individual human beings. We can only develop our distinctiveness because others keep telling us, in a variety of ways, how we appear to them. Certainly, at a crucial point (usually reached in our adolescent years) we have to make our own say about who we are, our own determination of what is true and what false in what other people tell us. But even this self-assertion should not take us apart from our most significant communities.

A vibrant ecclesiology would elaborate as richly as possible how a community, like a period of prayer to God, increases our proper individuality. Just as we become more ourselves, not less, by loving God more intensely and fulfilling the divine will more exactly, so we become more ourselves, not less, by participating in a healthy family or church. A healthy family wants us to flourish. A healthy church treasures our speaking out, offering our talents and wisdom, criticizing its deficiencies, bearing the burdens of its stupidity and sinfulness.

We are not ants or bees. Our participation in our communities ought to be aware, critical, chosen. Ultimately, all of us gain or miss fulfillment to the degree that we find love. We cannot find love if we insist on standing apart, refusing to be drawn into the richness, the complexity, indeed the messiness of relationships. Thus, men who want to find fulfillment, who realize they are aching for love as much as women are, ought to think well of relationships and try to work with others to make them flourish.

## 55. Are women naturally ordered to children?

Yes and no. Yes, in the obvious sense that women conceive children and bring children forth, while men cannot do this. Yes, in the related sense that, both throughout past history and today, women provide most of the care of children, most of the education that extends procreation. No, in the sense that many women feel no special affinity for children (feel less than what some men feel). No, in the sense that being born a female should not obligate a given woman to bear children, work with children, or make children a special factor in her life (beyond what all adults owe to the next generation, in terms of such matters as preserving the biosphere and providing excellent public education).

Nonetheless, both biology and socialization conspire to make women think about children more than men do. Girls are less able than boys to think about their futures apart from children. Any woman marrying has to calculate what conception will mean for her future, as any woman not marrying has to calculate what missing motherhood (or arranging for motherhood apart from marriage) will mean for her future. Men ought to make the same calculations, analogously, but the pressures on them to do so are lighter. For weal or woe, women are the potential bearers of the next generation. In that sense, they are naturally ordered to children and have to contend with the biblical maxim that childbearing impinges directly on their salvation (I Timothy 2:15, depending on Genesis 3:16).

### 56. Why can't women make up their minds?

If we take this question seriously, and not merely as a jibe, it draws us into the interesting complexity of at least stereotypically feminine consciousness. Women are the sex of both/and, not either/or. In this regard they are psychologically catholic rather than protestant. Seldom is their reality simple, black and white. Usually it is polychrome, dense, complex. Women see, and perhaps even more significantly feel, layer upon layer, connection upon connection. They are naturally ecological, relational, communitarian. Women's reality, like their work, tends never to be done. It is untidy, growing, evolving.

Does this come from greater contact with children—who are unpredictable and irrational—than what men tend to have? Does it stem from women's hormonal circularity, or their socialization to an outsider's privilege of watching for quirky, unsystematic particulars? A woman's eye supposedly notices details more readily than a man's. Women supposedly are more aware, more attuned to the complexity of what is going on around them, in both the natural and the social environments. Any of these characterizations breaks down if made a dogma, but each has its measure of probability. When one adds such measures of probability together, one has most of the answer to why women cannot make up their minds easily: the reality in which they are immersed does not admit of easy, simplistic choices.

This experience of reality relates to the stereotypic need of women to talk at length about a problem, go over and over its many aspects, before they can get it in perspective. The problem is seldom mathematically clear. If it impinges at all on real people, it is complex. Pull one thread of it and a quartet of further implications appears. Consider one course of action and immediately the unforeseeable response of the people to be acted upon steps forward to shadow one's path.

Men tend to solve this problem by cutting through contingencies and forcing the data to yield up a course of action. Inasmuch as men have been schooled by evolution to make the quick decisions necessary for success in hunting and warfare, their proclivity for ramming their way to an action makes sense. Women tend to be stuck or graced with the longer-playing problems: how to deal with an unhappy child, what to do about an unpleasant atmosphere at work, how to keep a changeable man reasonably happy. This can breed a useful but apparently slow, contemplative attitude: waiting for Godot, the resolver of irresolvable situations. It can also, less happily, bring women close to despair, or well into the thickets of indecisiveness, abulia. Thus, when mature women cannot make up their minds easily, painlessly, they are paying tribute to the murky, difficult complexities of reality itself.

## 57. Do feminists use stereotypes of men?

Yes, perhaps inevitably. To make the case that women require greater autonomy than what patriarchal cultures tend to grant them, feminists have to simplify what "patriarchal cultures" have been throughout history. In fact, all cultures have been shaped considerably by women, even if women's influence has come from what one might call the underside of history, the zones of the officially less powerful and less appreciated half of the race. It bears noting, of course, that women have tended to judge men the more powerful and appreciated half of the race, just as men have. Women have taken to heart the judgments of the cultures in which they have grown up, because such judgments have pressed upon them night and day. This does not mean that women in patriarchal cultures have hated themselves, but it does mean, as a generalization, that they have been more ambivalent about their sex than men have been about masculinity.

The most significant feminist stereotypes about men have it that men mature more slowly than women, think they are more rational than women but in fact are often more emotional, are more pigheaded than women, are less sensitive and concerned with relationships, and on average die younger than women because their greater aggression wears them out more quickly. Also, feminists tend to think that men are determined to cling to their privileges and so will not admit women to political, economic, religious, or other kinds of equality except as women pressure them to do so.

We all need stereotypes to make our way through the complexities of social life. We all sin against the complexity of social life by employing stereotypes clumsily, or by using them as clubs rather than delicate probes. Feminists tend to think that women are less liable to such sins than men, but sometimes that is a conceit rather than a reality. Ideological feminists harden themselves against the variety of men's views, the diversity of men's ways of proceeding in the world and treating women. Radical feminists make men the enemy *tout court,* simplistically.

Ideology is a plague, a profound form of dishonesty. It prejudges data and unconscionably separates people into two camps, the sheep and the goats. Certainly, all people have philosophical positions. However, honest people maintain positions that are corrigible—that further experience can correct, straighten out, give richer nuance. Ideologists seal themselves off from the correcting influences of further experience. At their worst, they become assassins—people so puffed up with a sense of commanding the truth that they will kill others (in reputation if not body) with nary a shiver. Men are probably more prone than women to this extreme of ideology, where one has to speak of fanaticism, but it remains a danger in circles of radical feminism, where anger calls more of the tunes than love.

### 58. Are women more sensitive than men?

This is another annoying question, because it seems to express an irritating simplicism. Certainly, the stereotype in many patriarchal cultures is that women have finer perceptions and feelings than men. Where men are trumpeted as more rational, women tend to be hymned as more sensitive. Reason becomes the province of men. Emotion becomes the province of women. This has had interesting consequences for religion.

Nineteenth century American culture, for example, made religion the sphere of women, conceiving religion as something delicate, emotional, refined—a zone that ought to dwell apart from the dirty hurly-burly of business and politics. In thinking this way, the mavens of the cultural day sought to limit the political impact of religious ideas. One powerful reaction was the Social Gospel movement, which insisted that the wretched conditions wrought by the industrial revolution were very much the business of the churches. Liberation theology is the heir of this Social Gospel movement, insisting that the biblical God wants, demands, social justice, just as the prophets of Israel tirelessly proclaimed. A counter-example is traditional Islam, where religious law was considered the height of rational prowess, women were excluded from religious scholarship, and women were then branded irreligious, unfit for attendance at the mosque or high communion with Allah.

A practical test for women's supposedly greater sensitivity than that enjoyed by men is whether women are more easily hurt by disparagement, neglect, lack of appreciation. On the whole, I find that women's socialization makes this the case. Many men are brought up to expect criticism—coaches yelling at them, fathers chewing them out. Whether this stems from a lingering military model of the education that males ought to receive, so that they be toughened for battle, or simply from men's impressions of what it takes to survive in male circles of various kinds (work, play, politics), it bothers many women, even when they throw up their hands and resign themselves that that is the way it is bound to be for their sons or brothers.

The problem becomes acute when men treat women with the brutality they are used to showing other men. Men may become uncomfortable at what they consider soft treatment from women, but often they enjoy it as much as they reject it. Few women enjoy harsh treatment, though perhaps many women sense after the fact that it has toughened them. Such a toughening can be good, inasmuch as women have to admit that in the world dominated by men they are going to come in for considerable abuse, but this "goodness" carries some pathetic overtones.

Why do any human beings have to brutalize others? Why are women so greatly pressured to move around men, slip by and "manage" men? The dishonesty that this entails is the dishonesty that emerged in our discussion of women's supposed manipulativeness. The women who chuckle at how easy it is to lead men around by the nose ought not to be happy late at night, when they should be examining their consciences. The abuse of good men that comes when women make fools of them for showing their affection nakedly, not defending themselves at all times, is nothing of which genuine feminists ought to be proud.

Thus "sensitivity" is another issue that unpeels like an onion. Little is simple about the relations between women and men; they are complicated, and also enriched, by millennia of slanted, somewhat dishonest interactions. For that reason, an escape into the rectifying simplicity of God that many religious traditions call heaven can beckon as a great relief. One day, all may be well, including the relations between supposedly brutal men and sensitive women.

## 59. Do feminists regularly criticize the male ego?

Yes. Feminists, and probably women in general, tend to be puzzled by male pride, male drive, male stubbornness, even when they can understand somewhat the evolutionary justification for these qualities. When it comes to matters such as warfare, feminists tend to stigmatize the male ego as a great source of evil and opine that, were women given half the say in running governments and military organizations, warfare would be far less frequent than it has been throughout history. This opinion comes to some grief when one contemplates the belligerence of a female political leader such as Margaret Thatcher, but feminists tend to dismiss Thatcher as an aberration—a woman who gained political power by blunting her best feminine instincts.

The besetting vice of the gilded women who do well in patriarchal cultures is often vanity. Vanity is no more attractive than pride, but the damage it does can seem less gigantic. Compared to the corpses strewn on the battlefield, the conceit oozing from the vain seems a sin of tiny proportions. The overarching pride of a Saddam Hussein, like the adamantine pride of an Ayatollah Khomeini, gives any sane person, but especially solid feminists, the willies. It seems so extreme as to call into question the person's mental balance. It also seems peculiarly male: a species of male fury, egotism, self-importance—call it what you will—that few women have been in the position to develop.

One may speak of the fury of the woman scorned, or tell fables of the unrivaled cruelty of the Amazons, but their actual conduct seldom brings women into the courts and jails. Men commit the vast majority of murders and crimes of violence. Men are the great engineers of war, as men are the presidents of most societies cruel enough to tolerate vast disparities between the rich and the poor. Behind all this male responsibility for evil lurks great egotism. Augustine (no mean student of egotism) spoke of sin as the love of self unto the contempt of God. Whether they realize it or not, the feminists who take aim at male egotism are shooting as Augustinians.

## 60. Are women more faithful than men?

This is an interesting question, especially if one hears nuances in its wording. First, statistics on infidelity in marriage seem to bear out the stereotype that more men than women are unfaithful. This raises questions about who the partners of such men are (as the moves of police against prostitutes raise questions about who the clients of prostitutes are), but it has yet to dent the stereotype that testosterone and ego drive the typical man to desire many sexual conquests. Similarly, women supposedly want stability more than variety—a single great love that grows deeper and deeper, to the point that it can support a whole family. Recently some popular sociologists of sexual mores have suggested that females are becoming as adulterous as males, but feminists have yet to accept this suggestion. A few feminists might defend the right of women to be as unfaithful as men, but most feminists who gain a significant hearing are mature enough to see that infidelity is always a moral failing.

A second overtone in the language of the question makes "faithful" bear on relations with God. Here it connects with a question we have already considered, whether women are more religious than men. Not to be repetitious, we need only point out that the answer to this question depends a great deal on how one regards religion. For the precise issue of faith (entrusting oneself to the mysterious God), the sociological data yield no solid indications. Faith escapes any easy, superficial evaluations. It includes the deepest motivations of the human heart, the deepest dramas, where people are saying yes or no to the lives God has meted out to them. Women may make fewer waves than men, break up fewer families, but whether this expresses a more frequent acceptance of divine providence is unclear.

All human beings have to respond to God day by day. Sufficient for any day is the evil thereof—and the challenge that such evil puts to faith. Neither men nor women will ever find it easy to reconcile a good God with the suffering that so many human beings have to endure. Many of these human beings are quite innocent, not deserving of hunger, homelessness, cancer, stroke, mental illness, poverty, earthquake, or any of the other horrors that life can thrust upon us. Whether men abandon themselves to God better than women, or women better than men, only God can say. Whether any given spouse will be more faithful to God than her or his partner reposes in the mercies of the divine mystery.

*Part IV:*

---

# ETHICAL ISSUES

### 61. What is ecofeminism?

Ecofeminism is the combination of feminist theory and environmentalism—advocacy of changes in the way we interact with the biosphere, because of what many commentators now call the "ecological crisis." In this combination, a feminist perception of the evils caused by a stereotypically masculine will to dominate others is extended to the environment, as a way of explaining why modern societies have so fouled their natural habitat. Ecofeminists think that the same patriarchal mentality that has led men to subjugate women has also led them to subjugate nature (significantly often conceived as feminine: Mother Earth). If we are to regain a sane ecological policy, we have to repent of the abuses that patriarchies have visited upon Mother Earth. We have to commit ourselves to new relations with nature, ones that are gentler, less intrusive, more reverent.

Some ecofeminists link these desirable new relations with a form of goddess religion, but most do not. Most are secular women appalled at the pollution of the skies, the chemical killing of the earth, the fouling of the waters. They see that the earth is dying. They realize that the earth is a living thing, a wonderfully vast organism that our industrial way of life has brought to its knees, choking and gasping. Why have we done this?

In the beginning, when technology first took aim at subduing nature (Bacon's notion that scientific knowledge is power comes to mind), the main reason was because we could do it. We were learning nature's secrets: finding ways to harness steam for power; methods to irrigate land, and then lay on pesticides, in order to increase the land's yield. It seemed foolish not to use this practical power, and using it brought a rush of pride, an intoxicating sense of accomplishment. Later we kept to our dominative ways, even when the evidence was piling up that these were killing the land and ruining the air, because we knew no better ways and enjoyed the comfortable material living that modern technologies afforded us.

Ecofeminists vary in the degrees to which they link a rejection of stereotypically male abuses of nature with a call for a simpler life-style, one that consumes fewer natural resources and encourages more spiritual pursuits. Secular ecofeminists can point to art, literature, research science, social services, and similar other pursuits that need not consume great amounts of natural resources. Religious ecofeminists can extol prayer and the appreciation of nature as a great gift of God. Together, both groups of ecofeminists can offer us a crucial insight: we have brought the same destructive mentality to nature that we have brought to many social situations. If we wish either to restore nature to good health or bring the world's peoples to peace, we need to jettison this mentality—repent and believe in the good (feminist) news that we only prosper by loving all our neighbors, human and nonhuman, as we love ourselves.

### 62. Why do feminists oppose dominion?

This question continues the line of inquiry raised by the question about ecofeminism. Feminists oppose dominion because it has caused their oppression. Men's desires to dominate women, control women, and keep women doing as men command, have caused women untold sufferings. Analogously, men's desires to subjugate nature have caused the sickening of nature, its battering and bruising. A will to power, dominion, is responsible for much poverty, illiteracy, bad health care, and despair, because it keeps the upper classes, the wealthy, from dealing with the middle and lower classes as equals, people just as human as themselves. Analyses of racism, ageism, ethnic biases, and even religious prejudices reveal that, among the many causes of these negative phenomena, a will to guard, if not increase, one's privileges stands high.

Genesis 1:26–30 expresses an early Israelite form of dominion. Human beings are put in charge of the earth, given the mandate to fill and subdue it. Certainly, one can argue that the full biblical message about the relations between human beings and the rest of earthly creation calls for men and women to be good stewards of creation. They ought to help all their fellow creatures to flourish. But throughout western history many developers who wanted to exploit nature have reached back to Genesis 1 for justification. Implicit in their cultural formation has been an image of the earth as wide open to human endeavor (a female ripe for exploitation, one is tempted to say).

As long as human technology was relatively simple, the devastation that our species could wreak on the forests and fields, and all wildlife, was relatively limited. From time to time early peoples destroyed their habitats, but their dominions were comparatively small. In modern times, however, our military, industrial, agrarian, maritime, and other technologies have given us enormous power over nature, as well as an enormous capacity to threaten less developed peoples. We have not visited upon either nature or other human beings all the wreckage that we might have, but we have done more than enough to show feminists the evils that patriachal societies have so regularly visited upon others, to control and to use "others" for their own profit, pleasure and pride. Because they find the relations between men and women in patriarchal cultures deeply flawed by this stereotypically male will to power, feminists can hate the word "dominion" and jam into it much of the evil that has warped human history.

### 63. Do feminists think ecologically?

Yes, I believe they usually do. What does it mean to think "ecologically?" It means to respect connections, relationships, interactions. It means to seek organic patterns, feel that the whole is more than the sum of its parts. Feminists may indeed be taught in universities how to analyze—the mental acts that take things apart to see how they are made and criticize them—but they tend to long for synthesis: putting things back together, learning how to build things up rather than break them down. The analytical mind has brought western higher education to debilitating heights of specialization. Professors have generated much more knowledge than wisdom. Feminists tend to be in the forefront of those lamenting this state of affairs. Proponents of women's studies (like proponents of religious studies) tend to argue that the entire educational enterprise should be interdisciplinary. Whatever helps to illumine a problem or clarify a phenomenon, is germane—history, literary analysis, philosophy, psychology, sociology, economics, biology, physics, religion.

This scholarly desire for interdisciplinary cooperation matches up well with the complexities, the ecological delicacies, of both the natural and social worlds. One cannot deal adequately with nature, for example, with even so familiar a phenomenon as a field of wheat, without knowing more than the biochemistry or physiology of plants. There are historical, aesthetic, and economic aspects to a field of wheat—what it was a hundred years ago, how it delights the eye and feeds the soul, how people are going to use its yield for bread, the staff of life—that cry out for understanding. Even on the level of natural science, there are complicated questions of what the side effects of the use of fertilizers will be, what animals move through the field, how different measures of sun and rain, heat or cold, will affect the wheat, the soil, the laborers. More and more, ecological science is encouraging us to assume an ecological mentality—a cognitional theory sensitive to connections. Reality is more like a spider's web than the straight lines of a train track. To think about reality well, we have to master shunts to the side as well as straight movements forward and back.

As we have seen in dealing with several previous questions, the stereotype is that women think more holistically, relationally, eco-logically than men. Feminists want to avoid the simplicities that can bedevil this perception while encouraging the advantages that it holds out. It would be better, more realistic and probably a great help toward peace, if both women and men thought more relation-ally in the future. It would be better if the stereotype of ecological thinking moved from the feminine mind to the simply human mind, wherever found.

#### 64. How can Mother Earth have rights?

This question keeps us within the orbit of ethical questions raised by the environmental crisis. "Mother Earth" is clearly a meta-phor, an image taken from human relations and imposed on nature. It is an obvious, nearly universal image, found across the span of traditional cultures. The earth is the source of food, the plants and animals on which human beings depend for survival. It is alive, a great womb. Many peoples have thought that Father Sky fertilized

Mother Earth, with sun and rain. The creativity of nature therefore reflected a cosmic sacred marriage.

The rights of Mother Earth in traditional cultures that cherished the mythology of such a sacred marriage included a claim to great reverence. One ought not to destroy any land wantonly. One ought to pay homage to the source of food, of life itself, with rites of Spring and Fall. One ought not to kill any of the children of Mother Earth, any of the animals one hunted or fished, without reluctance and reverence. Many traditional peoples developed complicated taboos, limiting how they could hunt or fish. Many took a part of the slain animal and returned it to the earth, that it might both find rest and regenerate—provide a new generation of deer or beavers.

In modern industrial times these ideas can seem quaint. Thus, it is less a reversion to mythological appreciations of nature, than a recoil at the damage done to the environment that prompts ecofeminists, and others, to argue that we should write into law rights for Mother Earth. The function of these rights would be to ensure the survival of nature: no defacing, abusing, exploitation, over-use that would kill any vital portion of the natural endowment. There should be no overhunting, overfishing, overfarming, overdevelopment that would inhibit a given area from remaining a source of food, recreation, and spiritual nourishment for future generations.

Few proponents of rights for nature reach a religious level, where one would write laws to protect natural areas because those areas were sacred. Few proponents think of nature as the medieval Christian scholastics could: as participating in the divine grant of existence that alone makes any creature be. One could bolster the arguments for nature's rights by taking such medieval concepts to mean that nature provides us with a presence of God—has an innate sacredness. Admittedly, one has to make one's way along this path cautiously, with several distinctions, but the path itself has solid theological justifications.

To abuse any creature is to act wrongly, in defiance of the divine intent at the heart of creation. Not to sense the sacredness of animals, rock faces, streams, and so not to restrain the egocentricity that causes us to slaughter, despoil, or pollute them, is to reveal a horrible blindness, a truly crippling irreligiousness. Thus, the further implications of the effort to establish rights for nature ought to interest all religious feminists. In our day Mother Earth can be considered the presence of a God as much feminine as masculine, a God who has chosen to be vulnerable throughout all creation, not simply in its human zones.


### 65. Is abortion the key feminist issue?

Many feminists seem to think that it is. For them, the epitome of patriarchal abuse is a woman's inability, legally and culturally, to control the use of her own body. Rape is one terrible form of such inability. Forcing women to bear children they do not want is another. Because few people approve of rape nowadays, even in cultures that remain heavily patriarchal, and while many people approve of restricting abortion, feminists can stake out abortion rights as their special battleground. I find this move understandable yet tragic.

Few women, including few feminists, favor abortion itself. Virtually all women abhor abortion and grieve for both mother and child. Abortion is usually a sign of failure—failure to plan, to discipline selfishness, to form a society with generous patterns of adoption, to develop successful programs of sex education and contraception, to support both women and men so that they succeed in marriage much more often than they fail. No one disputes the fact that the conceptus in a woman's womb is alive and on track to become a full human being. No one with any experience or sensitivity thinks that the typical woman carrying a fetus can view it impersonally, as though it were a cabbage in a shopping bag. The arguments put forward in favor of letting women decide whether they want to, feel that they can, carry a fetus to term boil down to the wisdom of letting the person most aware of the hazards and trials, the implications both negative and positive, have the key say.

This is a powerful position, but clearly not one invulnerable to further questions. If the fetus has a fully personal status—is already in the womb a special creation of God—then the fetus has formidable rights and it makes sense to wonder whether abortion isn't murder. If children are not merely the possessions of their mothers but also a gift and obligation to a wider community, then it makes sense to wonder whether the wider community should not have a say in a decision about abortion. Relatedly, what are the proper rights of fathers, who contribute half an infant's genetic endowment? To be sure, there are strong responses to each of these further questions, responses that amount to further defenses of a woman's right to make her own decision about abortion. Nonetheless, the further questions we have indicated, and many others that defenders of the fetus, opponents of abortion, can generate keep the entire matter complicated.

Moderate feminists tend to argue that a political position of pro-choice need determine none of the philosophical or theological matters involved in abortion, because this position does not oblige any woman to abort what she has conceived. This is a strong argument, but it does not shut down fully the rejoinder that if abortion is legal many women will avail themselves of it, which in numerous cases will be to sanction an irresponsible sex life or to refuse to face such matters as the personal status of the fetus and the obligation to reproduce oneself (meet our species's constant need for a next generation).

I see no end to reflections such as this, or to arguments such as the ones they imply. I sympathize with feminists who want to keep women from being chattel, pawns, less capable than men of controlling their own bodies, determining their own fertility. On the other hand, I find the secularism of some feminists chilling and the casual outlook of some abortionists deeply sinful. Probably few abortions are casual for the women undergoing them. Probably the majority are agonizing. Still, I wish feminists were more creative about ways to avoid abortion and less rigid about abortion rights. Thus I applaud feminist groups, such as my local chapter of Planned Parenthood, that emphasize education and contraception while not providing an abortion service.

### 66. How can feminists ignore the humanity of the fetus?

In the first place, most feminists do not ignore the humanity of the fetus. Most admit that the fetus is human, under way to becoming another woman or man. But many refuse to admit that the fetus is as human as the mother, or as other human beings living outside the womb. They will not call the fetus a person, and so they will not grant it personal rights, such as the right not to be terminated at the behest of another person, including one's own mother.

In the second place, many feminists shy away from an unblinking consideration of the status of the fetus because to do so would deflect them from their main goal, which is to defend the right of the woman involved to decide whether or not to carry the fetus to term. If one can avoid consideration of the status of the fetus one can more easily proceed as though the woman involved were simply seeking a neutral surgical "procedure," not significantly different from the removal of a cyst. How much bad will is involved in such an avoidance no outsider can say. Some women may believe sincerely that there is nothing profound to consider: they are carrying the fetus, it is theirs to dispose of as they wish. Other women may be shielding themselves from a strong intuition that if they ever looked closely at the fetus it would become their child—something quite personal.

The more advanced the pregnancy, the more obvious becomes the childlike, personal quality of the fetus. The more we learn about fetal development, the more impressed we are likely to be with the humanity of the conceptus, even with its individuality. Still, it is not clear that the normal development of a fetus entitles us to call it personal from the moment of conception. To come to that judgment, one probably needs a conviction of faith that God cooperates from the moment of conception to give the fetus a sacred status (whether we should call this status a "soul" can be debated). Lacking such a conviction of faith, many feminists find it relatively easy to consider the first phases of a pregnancy—for example, the first trimester—the production and evolution of something less than fully human.

### 67. Do feminists ignore the seamless garment of life?

Yes, many appear to do so. The "seamless garment" of life is a figure used by Cardinal Joseph Bernardin of Chicago to link abortion, capital punishment, euthanasia, warfare, and other ethical matters bearing on the value of human life. Feminists may ignore or reject this figure for several reasons.

First, their concern with abortion may blind feminists to the parallels between this ethical matter and the others just mentioned. Second, they may not possess the philosophical sophistication necessary to see the thread of sameness running through all these matters. Third, they may not consider human life sacred, and so they may take relativistic positions on any of these questions. For example, they may admit capital punishment under many circumstances, see little wrong with euthanasia or even suicide in certain cases, accept warfare as a sorry regularity in human history, or think that abortion destroys a prepersonal life and so is little different from the destruction of a litter of unwanted kittens. I am not saying that any feminists hold all of these views, or even that a majority would subscribe to any one of them. I am simply saying that the notion of a seamless garment includes the unexpressed judgment that the entire matter covered by the garment (human life) is sacred.

We know that consistency can be the hobgoblin of little minds. We also know that mature people tend to strive for consistency, want to be rational rather than simply impulsive. Somewhere between these two insights lies the field that most human beings, including most feminists, tend to plow. On the one hand, they want the right to distinguish between different species of evil, in this case different species of possible murder—wrongful taking of human life. On the other hand, they want to have solid reasons for their views on any of the questions involved—euthanasia, capital punishment, the others.

To pass from vague feelings to solid reasons can be difficult and painful. Often people not trained in ethical reasoning can conclude that they are better off simply following their primitive instincts. Many feminists, though sophisticated in other areas, are not trained in ethical reasoning. Thus the appeal of a seamless garment, and the possibility of arguing for it persuasively, escape them. They make do with a patchwork ethics, and a few of them even glorify this making do, calling it how women think—with an aversion to the "consistency" or "reasonableness" that men laud.

## 68. Should women be sovereign over their own bodies?

We have glanced at this question in earlier reflections on abortion. The answer that I find most balanced is a qualified yes.

Women should be as sovereign over their bodies as men are, provided that women's capacity to conceive and carry children does not establish a critical difference. If women are as human as men, they should enjoy the sovereignties that men enjoy. In the present instance, they should, for example, receive the same reverence and autonomy in the matter of medical care. If women should be able to buy a car or a house, to sell a piece of their land or some of their furniture, with the same sovereignty as men, all the more should they be able to make decisions about their own bodies.

However, if we believe that we have not made ourselves but come from God, God has rights over our entire existence. God may principally desire that we grow freer and freer, but this can entail the perception by lawful religious authorities that we ought not to commit suicide or practice euthanasia. It may entail the arguably similar perception that we ought not to abort our fetuses.

Here the biological difference of women from men becomes a matter of capital significance. Men cannot carry fetuses and so cannot contemplate abortion as women can. The closest that a man can come is contemplating the destruction of the life that his wife or lover has conceived by him. A man can find such a contemplation wracking. However, it can never become the contemplation of an action to occur in his own body, to bring the destruction of life beating under his own heart. I believe that this difference suggests that women ought to have more say than men in abortion, as in conception. I do not believe that this difference settles the matter of whether women ought to be completely sovereign in either matter.

As noted previously, the human community and the woman's spouse (to a lesser extent, her lover) have a legitimate interest in procreation and so in abortion. For the moment we may disregard the interest of the human community at large, because there is no scarcity of births worldwide. We may not disregard the interest of the woman's spouse, because procreation is at the heart of the marital relationship, along with making love and sharing overall destiny. This does not mean that all spouses are required to procreate, that all women are required to conceive. Alone, it does not settle the matter of what responsibility a woman has to carry a fetus to term. But it does indicate a let, a limit, on a woman's sovereignty over her body. I believe that a woman who has conceived cannot rightly claim the entire say in a decision about abortion. I believe that in a good marriage the spouses will work out such a decision together, the man realizing that the woman has more at stake and the woman wanting to discern and honor the wishes of her husband, if at all possible.

### 69. What is womanist thought?

My impression is that womanist thought is feminist thought shaped especially by considerations of race, but perhaps also by considerations of class and ethnic background. Black feminists have been the driving force behind womanist thought, arguing that white feminists tend to overlook important factors in women's oppression, concentrating only on women's control by men. For example, white women tend to overlook the ways in which they themselves have participated in the subjugation of African-American women and enjoyed ill-gotten gains from it.

Womanist thought therefore has been an elevator raising up the complexity of women's actual lives. If we are to deal with how women actually live, we cannot separate sexism from racism, economics, questions of class, questions of ethnic status, and questions of religion. All of these interact to produce the actual conditions under which a given woman has to compose her life. The income a woman has, what her religious group tells her about her sex, how people of other religious, economic, ethnic and racial classes (women as well as men) interact with her—all of these shape her actual life. In many cases, each of these factors brings to mind historical grievances; any may therefore imply the need for confrontation, repentance, reconciliation.

For example, African-American feminists may feel that they cannot stand shoulder to shoulder with white feminists until their past subordination to white women, in the starkest case as slaves, is acknowledged and the two groups work through it. Similarly, African-American feminists may feel that what white women say about the patterns of subjugation they have suffered does not fit what African-American women have experienced with African-American men. To assume that patriarchy has meant the same thing in both cases could be to depreciate the distinctiveness of African-American culture. It could be a case of the majority, in this case white women, simply assuming that their experiences were valid for the minority. Womanist thought is therefore a strong reminder that feminists cannot be simpleminded even about women's oppressions by men. It has become as well, a strong way for Black women to reflect on the strengths and weaknesses of their own particular traditions.

### 70. How do feminists regard race?

This question continues the lines of reflection raised by the question about womanist thought. Feminists open to womanist thought (no doubt, the majority) now tend to regard race as an important social factor, a key ingredient in what either feminism or sexism ought to mean. Womanist thought, along with its analogies in ethnic considerations, in the matter of sexual orientation, in economic issues, and in matters of class (high culture or low, linked with advanced education or limited), has been pushing feminist thought in the direction of pluralism. The current orthodoxy is that one ought to think, write, interpret in the plural. The present preference is to spotlight diversity rather than similarity, let alone uniformity.

I find this emphasis salutary, inasmuch as it brings home the rich variety, even the considerable conflict, that we find in women's lives, women's interactions. However, I also suspect that some of it is a temporary emphasis, bound to lessen if women are going to be able to cooperate and deal effectively with the problems they share simply by being females.

Black women and white women, or Hispanic women, live different lives because of their racial, cultural, economic, sexual, and perhaps religious orientations. Race is only one of the several leading indicators of their dissimilarity and the distance they have to travel if they are to understand one another. This is not to say it is a minor matter. Inasmuch as race has a tragic history in the United States and has become a major force in the formation of the black and white subcultures, feminism neglects race at its peril.

Still, there are experiences that women share across the racial and ethnic spectrum (for example, childbirth, menstruation, menopause, vulnerability to rape), as there are experiences that women share with men because they are similarly black, or Catholic, or Jewish, or unemployed. Feminists, therefore, face the wonderful, staggering task of expanding their awareness and sympathy so that these become as universal as possible. Whatever helps to clarify the message that women are as fully human as men, and to forward the causes that that message implies for politics, economics, and other fields, ought to be attractive to genuine feminists.

### 71. How do feminists regard class?

Here positions may vary considerably, but my impression is that the majority of American feminists, who are white and middle class, realize that differences in economic status and education cause significant differences in how women hear the word "feminism."

Just as opposition to smoking tends to break down along lines of income and class, so that people from the lower classes smoke considerably more than people from the middle and upper classes, so openness to feminism is in good measure a function of a woman's income and education. Lower class women tend to regard feminism as a luxury they cannot afford. They need all the help they can get from the establishment, the patriarchy. They are well aware that they suffer sexual discrimination, but they doubt that organizing to protest it, let alone coming together to develop a women's spirituality or politics, would justify the time or energy it would require.

Upper class women can use their independence to become ardent feminists, but the majority do not. The majority are likely to possess their advantages through their husbands or fathers, and to favor the patriarchal status quo. Like lower class women, they are well aware that many men patronize them, but generally they are sufficiently insulated to render such patronage more irritating than threatening.

Middle class women may shy away from feminism if they expect it to entail an aggressiveness or constant complaining that jars with the femininity they want for themselves, their daughters, their nieces and granddaughters. They may also recoil if they fear that feminism is dominated by lesbianism, as may women from the lower or higher classes. But when they have informed themselves sufficiently to realize that feminism can mean simply the conviction that women are as fully human as men and the commitment to promote this equality, middle class women become the field ripest for harvest. The middle class is the majority of the population. It is responsible for running the great national systems: education, medicine, science, the military, government, much of the economy. Thus, in the measure that feminism wins the allegiance of middle class women, and also middle class men, it will have secured the essential victory.

### 72. Is ethnicity important to feminists?

Yes, increasingly so. In the United States, one finds the beginnings of a Hispanic and an Asian feminism. Abroad, one finds strong feminists in many of the European countries, and sparks of feminism on the other continents. The strength of patriarchy in a given culture tends to determine the difficulties that feminists must surmount. Nonetheless, there are Muslim feminists, Japanese feminists, Latin American feminists, and African feminists.

A major problem in developing feminism outside the west is the perception, or the charge, that feminism is the product of western cultures. Thus, the leaders of traditional African or Asian cultures can lump feminism with colonialism, and argue that the preservation of native traditions requires the rejection of feminism. Muslim women, for example, can be torn between taking to heart a system of analysis that seems likely to illumine their cultural condition, and defending the only way of life that they have known. If the male leaders of their culture tell them that feminism is a product of the Great Satan, they have to be unusually independent to embrace feminist analyses.

We are all the products of the cultures that form us, and those cultures are themselves the result of many forces. Race, religion, ethnicity, economics, and politics interact with sex and numerous other realities that are matters of both fact and interpretation. It may be a physical fact that I am a woman of such and such height, weight, age, education, ill or good health. However, how I think about my womanhood is as important as the physical facts that specify it.

Ethnicity is doubly complicated in a composite society such as the United States (though nowadays few geographical areas do not house at least composite subpopulations. Consider, for example, the divide between Sunnis and Shiites in Iraq, to say nothing of the influence of the Kurds.) At what point does a person become an "American" without a hyphen? Certainly my grandparents were Irish-Americans. Probably my parents also were. But it is not clear that I am. I have visited Ireland, but I have never lived there. I belong to no Irish-American societies, frequent no exclusively Irish-American gatherings. I have Irish-American friends, but probably they are not the majority. I think of myself as a middle-class American of Irish and Catholic background, but constantly I am dealing with people of different religious and ethnic backgrounds. Thus any Irishness in my ethnicity is muted. I would not deny its autobiographical force beneath the surface, and I take a warm pride in many aspects of this heritage, but it does not color my days as overtly as an African or Asian or Hispanic or even Jewish heritage would. The pluralistic trend of current feminist studies seeks to honor ethnicity and other forces shaping women's lives, but precisely what this will mean for future political cooperation remains to be seen.

## 73. Is there a politically correct feminism?

No, not in a strict sense, though the majority of feminists turn out to be liberal in their politics, secular in their values, pro-choice in the matter of abortion, heterosexual but supporters of rights for gays and lesbians, and liberal regarding the rights of racial and ethnic minorities. What any of these tags means for a given feminist has to be determined on the spot. "Liberal" is so vague a term as to be useful only to the simple-minded (and so to dominate political advertising in my part of the country at election time). "Conservative" is no better. There are a few conservative feminists, but they are an anomaly, inasmuch as feminism mounts a radical challenge to the status quo. There are a few feminists opposed to abortion, but they usually feel themselves to be a distinct minority.

Thus, "political correctness," de facto, amounts to an expectation among mainstream feminists that others claiming the feminist label will favor democratic, egalitarian movements that promote women's opportunities and square well with similar movements among blacks, Asians, homosexuals, and the handicapped. On the whole, feminists expect that those who have become conscious of women's oppressions will be alert to similar oppressions of other groups (most of which will number women) and so will vote, try to move public opinion, and perform the other acts that we call "political" with a preferential option for the poor, the underdogs, those struggling to get a fair shake.

## 74. Does feminism give special privileges to lesbians?

Many lesbians are attracted to feminism, because it promotes the cause of women's liberation, women's progress toward full equality of opportunity with men. However, the majority of feminists are not lesbians but heterosexuals—straights. Thus, the majority of feminists want to interact with men, love men, collaborate with men, co-opt men to the feminist movement, because this majority is attracted to good men and sees humanity as irreducibly two-sexed. Lesbians may or may not be able to second many of these instincts and judgments. They may or may not have good male friends. Understandably, straight feminists tend to favor lesbians who interact with men well, even if such straights honor the rights of more radical, angry or isolationist lesbians to go their own way.

Inasmuch as it implies a fierce love of women and exaltation of women's ways, lesbianism can claim to be the purest feminism— what all women might see and feel, if patriarchy had never formed their psyches. This is a debatable claim, on both biological and psychological grounds, but it has been sufficiently powerful to generate the phenomenon sometimes known as "political lesbianism": straight women separating from men and consorting mainly with women out of a conviction that the oppression of women requires a complete commitment to change, if women are ever to see its demise. Political lesbians may or may not become physical lovers of other women. Their stance is sufficiently radical, though, to make them strong proponents of the general lesbian bias that, in the current situation, lesbians are the women most free of patriarchal fetters. This is not the standard or most influential feminist line, but it deserves a patient hearing from feminist intellectuals.

### 75. How does feminism regard pornography?

Balefully. The heaviest damage of pornography falls on women. Even though men are corrupted by the excitation of their lust and there are pornographies directed to heterosexual and lesbian women as well as to homosexual men, pictures of women provide the focus of the pornographic mainstream. (I omit consideration of "kiddie porn," which brutalizes both girls and boys.) Pornography teaches men to regard women as objects of lust, pleasure, convenience. It dehumanizes women, and so men, by making men carnal, blind to spiritual values, creatures bent on rut rather than love. The women co-opted into pornography are often also co-opted into prostitution. In both cases, economic need tends to be the main cause.

Women sell their bodies, and so goodly portions of themselves, because their culture seems to offer them few alternatives. If they have little education, poor job skills, and little self-esteem, they are fair game for both pornographers and pimps. The vast majority are young, in their teens. They know little, are alone, afraid, defenseless. Feminists, therefore, tend to regard pornography as another vicious face of patriarchy. Along with rape and prostitution, pornography establishes patriarchy as an oppressive hydra with several heads to be severed.

The feminism with which I am familiar, to which I am loyal, pays little attention to theoretical arguments that try to establish the rights of women to sell their bodies or enjoy a pornography that exploits men. Feminists should try to rehabilitate "lust," if they want to throw out prudery and deal with sexual desire honestly, but this is not the lust stigmatized in the traditional ethical manuals, not the lust making pornography a multibillion-dollar industry. Sexual desire is natural, healthy, good. Certainly, it requires certain conditions to be moral. It ought to be the servant of love. So it is "lust" only in the sense that it is erotic, itching and burning for the pleasure of union with the beloved. It need not depersonalize the beloved, and it has no traffic with sales, money, the debasement of the body of either the one viewed or the voyeur.

The women I know experience sexual desire holistically. They are less split than men, less enticed by copulation with a stranger whose only known merits are physical—muscles or curves. So pornography seems to them debasing, inhuman, a regression from the health, the maturity, they enjoy fairly naturally. Feminism tends to assume this holistic orientation and the maturity it confers. Few feminists are saints, spiritual to the degree that bodily matters are of no interest. Many feminists, in fact, would disagree with such a traditionally Christian view of saintliness, if "saintliness" is supposed to name anything profoundly human, universally admirable, arguing that we all have the obligation to transform the world, honor our bodies, take a rightful pleasure in creation.

Nonetheless, the mainstream of feminist thought and practice, as I observe it, is sufficiently spiritual to abhor the carnal, low, lewd character of pornography. Pornography is offensive, aethestically as well as morally and religiously. It represents what feminists want to veto, render inoperative and unnecessary. It feeds on the worst human drives and exploits the weak. So it is an enemy, or a sadly, offensively representative face of the patriarchal enemy. Thus, feminists might say to pornography what Jesus said to Peter, when Peter was being stupid about the ways of God: "Get thee behind me, Satan" (Mark 8:33).

## 76. How does feminism tend to analyze domestic violence?

Domestic violence seems to many feminists a logical result of patriarchal ideology. If men believe that they have the right, indeed the obligation, to control women, it makes a perverted sense for men to beat women into submission. The biblical portrayal of wives as submissive to their husbands sows the seeds of this illogic, as does the biblical maxim about sparing the rod and spoiling the child. I believe that neither maxim justifies physical abuse, but I have spoken with battered women in shelters who not only saw the Bible as the source of their husbands' claim to beat them but also thought that claim legitimate. Indeed, the harsh punishments imposed in the Pentateuch have told both Jewish and Christian men that they can discipline women as need requires. The case is similar for Muslim women, inasmuch as the Qur'an (4:34) can be read as instructing husbands to punish disobedient wives physically.

Generally, men are larger and physically stronger than women. Generally, men can beat women with relative impunity. Therefore, when men do not regard women as their equals, and as images of God, women live in peril. Certainly, many men adopt an attitude of *noblesse oblige,* considering the vulnerability of women reason to treat them gently, even to act protectively. But this attitude turns out to be fragile. If women do not show themselves docile, grateful for such protection, the next time they prove irritating they can get the back of the man's hand.

Often men who abuse their wives and children protest that they do not want to act this way, do not understand why they lash out physically. Their lives have made them unhappy. They are full of resentment and bitterness. So they vent their spleen on those around them, largely because they can. Until women and children find ways to escape such men, either to flee or to stand up to them, little is likely to change. Certainly, therapy helps some men, but a man has to be quite sick to batter the people of his own household on a regular basis. Such sickness does not yield to quick cures. Indeed, and sadly, often the abusive spouse or parent is merely repeating patterns that he (or she) suffered as a child. Thus domestic violence can go on generation after generation: the fathers have eaten sour grapes, so the children's teeth are set on edge.

The feminist solution to domestic violence usually entails two steps. First, those being abused must remove themselves, or be removed, from the abusive situation. Second, education and reform, as wide and deep as possible, have to overturn the pervasive patriarchal attitudes that give disturbed men license to beat their wives and children. The first step requires establishing havens, safe houses, shelters—call them what you will. There must be places in each city to which abused women and children can flee. The second step is dauntingly difficult, a matter for the very long haul. Until the feminist revolution overturns patriarchy fully, most men are not going to accept the equal humanity of women. They may temporize, accommodate, push their prejudices underground, but any upset is going to tempt them to take their frustrations out on their wives and children, either physically or verbally.

### 77. Do any feminists oppose contraception?

Very few. The data on the population explosion, the arguments in favor of women's being able to control their own fertility, and the horrors of abortion combine to persuade most feminists that sex education and contraception are crucial to the well-being of both women in particular and society in general. Few women accept the natural law theory on which most prohibitions of contraception are based. Equally few accept the proposition that sexual intercourse can be sacrificed without harming the love between spouses. For weal or woe (more weal than woe, I believe), women, along with western culture generally, now insist that sexual love should not be held suspect, considered the foe of spiritual development, kept in the closet as an embarrassment. Precisely those attitudes have led us to the current pass, where a balanced attitude toward sexuality is hard to find.

On the one hand, repressive teachers would keep us fearful of sexual love, making it difficult to enjoy what ought to be both a splendid gift of God and a powerful help in people's struggles to be good spouses and parents. On the other hand, permissive teachers and popular figures are trying to sell a gospel of salvation through license—fulfilling every erotic desire, acting out every fantasy. The path of virtue lies in the middle. If contraception is essential to walking this path and making it viable for the majority, then contraception is not only legitimate but mandatory.

We have to limit the number of births. We have to be able to separate physical lovemaking from procreation, even as we insist that overall the two belong together. It may not be necessary to keep every act of intercourse open to procreation. Practically, it is probably not possible without ruining the world demographically and most relationships psychologically. If women cannot control their fertility, they face two choices that most are going to consider unacceptable. Either they abstain or they accredit abortion. Abstinence has its place, but so does intercourse. In most cases, acknowledging the place of intercourse means resorting to contraception, because the only fully safe alternative is an abstinence so complete as to vitiate the rights of intercourse. Without the provision and use of simpler alternatives, abortion becomes a contraceptive. Most feminists find this repellent and so promote ordinary contraception as the part of simple sanity.

### 78. How do feminists regard gun control?

As another matter of simple sanity—most feminists recoil from violence. Whether it be domestic, military, or criminal, violence clashes with women's usual upbringing, perhaps even with women's usual biology (which is oriented to nurturing children and protecting them). The obvious place of guns in violence makes guns women's enemy. Most women feel little attraction to hunting, though many can find a limited place for such sport. Most women are also repelled by violent crime and warfare. Thus guns almost always carry negative connotations. The multitudes killed each year in gang clashes, crimes, and hunting accidents are all children of women—sons, daughters, brothers, sisters, husbands, and lovers. Guns, therefore, can epitomize the craziness of patriarchal cultures, which enables even weak men to slaughter and maim.

Why is there so much anger in men? Why is there so much irrationality? When women note that men belonging to the National Rifle Association oppose even minimal restrictions on the purchase of guns, they tend to throw up their hands in despair. Similarly, feminists cannot believe that healthy people could oppose the Brady Bill, generated to avoid tragedies like that visited on President Reagan's press secretary. That Presidents Reagan and Bush could oppose it only makes their rule appear "political" in the worst of senses, the most prostituted of ways. Like the mothers who have mobilized against drunk driving, the feminists who support gun control think that they are acting directly in everybody's best interest, not the least that of the women whom guns leave bereft. The fewer guns available to angry, violent men, the fewer tragedies there will be to set women keening.

### 79. Are feminists internationalists?

Not necessarily, though logically they should be. The more women learn about their sisters in other cultures, the more sympathy they tend to feel. Across considerable cultural divides, similar abuses and sufferings stand out clearly. The Muslim women draped in *chadors* and veils may be directed by men more dramatically than western women, but western women can point to the softer tyranny their own culture imposes when it comes to dress, fashion, the control and display of their sexuality. African women suffering genital mutilation tend to raise in western women both horror and sympathy, in part because alert western women find analogies in the elective cosmetic surgery that puts their domestic sisters at risk. Everywhere, women are the majority of the poor. Everywhere, women have the primary care for children, are vulnerable to rape and beating, have the lesser voice in politics and business, can find even religion a source of oppression.

The more that feminists gather in international assemblies, the more they will dispel both the myth and the reality that feminism is a western creation, affecting only women in North America and Europe. Obviously women in other geographical areas have to adapt western ideas and practices to their own native situations. Certainly they have to work out for themselves what is needed to progress toward political, religious, economic, and other kinds of equality. But it flies in the face of women's experience, both direct and vicarious, to say that feminism is not an international movement, issue, cause. Wherever there is the patriarchal subjugation of women to men, the patriarchal argument that women are the second sex, feminists find fertile ground. As the world becomes smaller, through increased communication and quicker travel, women everywhere are discovering their links with sisters far and near.

## 80. Are feminists conservationists?

Again, not necessarily, though conservationism, like internationalism, seems to be a natural ally of, or have an affinity to feminism. As ecofeminism suggests, some feminists have found close links between environmentalism and the women's movement. The domination of women and the domination of nature both appear to be products of the aberrant patriarchal mind. Similarly, an ecological mentality, sensitive to the connections among beings, the webs connecting creatures within a holistic habitat, appeals to most women, as though their socialization made it connatural. Most women want to think relationally. Most tend to judge matters in terms of both/and rather than either/or. The models that most appeal to mainstream feminists are communitarian, cooperative, democratic. Typically feminists recoil from hierarchies and pyramids, preferring circles. All of this suggests an inclination to ecology and so, in the present historical instance, to conservation.

When we study the current state of the biosphere, we realize that the ecological crisis stems largely from a lack of restraint. Everywhere people are trying to exploit nature. As we have begotten more people, and prolonged life considerably, the human race has begun to consume more than what nature can provide without sickening. The "carrying capacity" of nature is coming within sight. Already we are asking for more than is sane. Already our destructive way of life in the developed nations seems unnatural, the enemy of both Mother Earth and posterity.

People whose consciousnesses have been raised so that they can discern women's oppression by patriarchal patterns of thought, generally find it easy to understand these charges. On the whole, it makes sense to them that we cannot dominate nature as we have done in the past, because this treatment has put nature in peril. If we are to change our ways, we have to simplify our lives. We have to consume less materially and demand more spiritually. Religious feminists often realize that this imperative presents a wonderful opportunity. If we can show people that spiritual pursuits such as art, research science, higher education, prayer, music, and the like fulfill them more than overeating, overtraveling, overdressing, and the other vices of consumerist societies, we can both ease the assaults on nature and provide our people with more happiness.

Happiness does not come from accumulating more and more possessions, working for an ever bigger home. Social justice requires that the needs of the many take priority over the wants of the few. The wealthy citizens of the developed countries are the few. The poor of the developing countries are the many. If the goods of the earth exist for all the earth's people, as Christian social teaching has long proclaimed, then feminists, indeed all people of alert conscience, should gladly call themselves conservationists, and gladly be such in fact.

*Part V:*

---

# THE CHURCH AND FEMINIST SPIRITUALITY

## 81. How do Christian feminists want to be treated?

In the spirit of Paul's conviction expressed in Galatians 3:18, Christian feminists want to be treated as though in Christ there were neither male nor female. "In Christ" is Paul's regular shorthand for the exalted and corporate character of Christian existence. Believers are united with one another through their union with Christ, who is a living spirit. Paul has in mind the resurrected Lord, active in the midst of his people, because they are freed by his resurrection to live in the time when God is all in all. Compared to the splendid new creation that faith gives them, by incorporating them into Christ, believers should find their social differences almost trivial. They may be rich or poor, free or slave, Jew or Gentile, but in Christ their status does not matter crucially. Nor does their sex. What matters crucially is their faith. They are all members of the one body of Christ. Each has her or his role to play. Each ought to realize that every other member makes an irreplaceable contribution.

The so-called deutero-pauline literature (the letters probably written by disciples rather than Paul himself, such as the Pastorals, Colossians, and Ephesians) renege on this vision of equality. For them, existence in Christ does not jar with a hierarchical structuring of social relations. Then whether one is female or male matters considerably, because wives are subordinate to their husbands, as their husbands are subordinate to Christ. This analogy, developed in Ephesians 5, is doubly pernicious. First it subjugates women to men, as though men were more human or holy than women. Second it implies that men are more like Christ—are "heads" by participation in the headship of Christ.

Christian feminists do not want to be treated in this deutero-pauline way. They do not want to receive the ministrations of what Elisabeth Schüssler-Fiorenza has called a "love patriarchy." They want the full political power of the gospel unleashed, so that dominative, hierarchical structures are blown away. They deny that treating slaves lovingly justifies retaining a slave system. Equally, they deny that treating women lovingly justifies a patriarchal system.

Jesus was a radical, politically. Saying this may upset conservative people, but one has only to read the gospel straightforwardly to
find it obvious. Jesus opposed the religious and political establish-
ments of his day. The reign of God that he announced greatly relativ-
ized the claims of both priests and procurators. Jesus preferred the
poor to the rich, outcasts like tax-collectors and whores to the
righteous. He made friends with women and admitted them as disciples—something rare, almost unheard of for a rabbi of his time.
Christian feminists want to be treated the way that Jesus treated
women. They want respect, equal opportunity, the right to be themselves. In the church for which they long, they would be invited to
contribute their talents, to lead and to serve, just as enthusiastically
as men. Their daughters would serve at the altar just as readily as
their sons. Any of their children could be priests and bishops, if
inclination and talent warranted. Indeed, they themselves could
aspire to be priests, mediators between God and human beings,
because in Christ wisdom weighed more heavily than sex and patriarchal biases.

### 82. Do we need a women's Bible?

Yes, though not precisely what Elizabeth Cady Stanton created
more than a hundred years ago. Cady Stanton followed Marcion,
Martin Luther, Thomas Jefferson, and other eminent predecessors
in excising scriptural materials that she felt jarred with either the
genuine message of Jesus or the dignity of women. I believe that
women should not excise anything from the received, canonical
text, but that they should emphasize the texts that show the equality
of women with men under God and criticize acutely the texts that
reveal a patriarchal bias at odds with such an equality.

The Bible is a human document. No matter what theory of
inspiration one holds, the patent fact is that the Bible has come into
human culture in a language and collection of thought-forms indebted to particular times, peoples, and places. Not even the most
hidebound, literalist, infallibilist theories of biblical interpretation
can get around the fact that the biblical God "wrote" in Hebrew and

Greek rather than Hindi and German. But language is only the tip of the iceberg. Beneath it, coming to point in and through it, lies the entire spiritual stance of the people who coin it, use it, adapt it. Thus, biblical Hebrew is the medium of a given people's soul, as biblical Greek is the medium of another people's soul.

Neither of these "peoples" is monolithic. Each is rich and diverse. Nonetheless, compared to the peoples who have understood themselves through the Arabic of the Qur'an or the Sanskrit of the Vedas, the biblical peoples have been unmistakably distinct. Their scriptures have been particular, even parochial, as well as universal. Only the pejoratively simple could think such scriptures would not be fallible in matters not crucial to salvation.

Patriarchal biases against women, which mar both testaments of the Christian scripture (for example, consult the laws of the Torah and the deutero-pauline letters), are not crucial to salvation. Indeed, they obscure salvation, making it hard for half the race to believe that God has delivered the definitive grace of Christ into the hands of sinful church leaders. Unless feminists can exhibit mature, critical minds and distinguish between what is corrigible in the scriptural deposit of faith, and what must stand unchanged, they have to withdraw from the whole venture of taking the Bible as the word of God.

God cannot be a patriarchal sexist. The predicate, implying defect and sin, cannot be linked with the subject. Those who want God to determine what is and is not sin put forward a worthy desire, but they err grievously, mortally, if they equate the bare words on the received biblical record with the determinations of God. Who can believe that it honors God, credibly stems from God, to require women to keep silent in church when men can speak? Who can believe that Eve is more culpable for the woes of humanity than Adam (letting the myth stand for the mystery of human fallenness)? Women have suffered terribly from both of these New Testament propositions. How can God be the author of such injustice? How can God not be the enemy of interpretations of the biblical text that prop up a male supremicism? Women need a biblical interpretation that defends them against an incredible God. They need to pry biblical interpretation, preaching the word of God, away from patriarchs who want to keep women in an inferior place. In all these senses,

they need a women's Bible: one that is as liberating for their own sex
as for men.

### 83. Should churches ordain women?

Yes and no. Yes, the day should be with us, upon us, when the
churches that presently do not ordain women agree that women can
be as fit for ordination to ministry as men and so can ordain women
with great joy. The time should be fulfilled when women are welcomed to priestly service as gladly, as enthusiastically, as compara-
bly gifted men, so that the ordination of women is a cause for rejoic-
ing and goes forward with complete legal and cultural fittingness.

No, church leaders should not ordain women illicitly. Even
when it might be arguable, for example, that a Catholic bishop's
ordaining a woman would be valid (despite the fact that the qualifi-
cations for priestly ordination now set forth in canon law stipulate
that the candidate be male), doing this illicitly would place such
women in the shade and make them a cause of division in the Catholic and Orthodox churches. Those who argue that change only
comes by breaking repressive laws are worth hearing, but their argument misfires in the context of the church, where feminist believers
of any depth have to want a politics different from what obtains in
secular societies, a politics worthy of the dignity of all believers as
members of Christ's body.

Certainly, more than cynical feminists have concluded that
male powerholders in the Roman and Eastern Orthodox churches
will continue to cling to their privileges, lamentably failing to distinguish themselves from their self-serving secular brothers, and so that
such powerholders will have to be dragged to the ordination of
women kicking and screaming. Certainly, it is a dreary fate to contemplate only the near collapse of the Catholic sacramental system,
long its great pride and supposed reason for the priesthood to be, as
finally forcing Roman and Orthodox leaders to ordain women (and
Roman leaders to ordained married men). Still, in my opinion none
of this justifies a collusion of feminists and outlaw bishops to divide

the church and foul the memory of the Johannine Jesus who prayed so movingly that all his people be one (John 17).

## 84. Should female religious be autonomous?

Yes, as autonomous as male religious. No religious, no priests, not even any laity can desire a complete autonomy. All have to submit to Christ, and to accept the limits that have inevitably, legitimately arisen as the community of Christ articulated itself throughout history. The church of Christ exists in time and space. It embraces real, limited people. Inevitably, it is political, for good as well as bad. Religious exist to serve the church and the world. They enjoy a mode of life sanctioned by the church—called holy, because it has shown holy fruits. Monks and nuns have applied to the church for admission into this sanctioned life of holiness. It makes sense, therefore, that they should continue to take direction from lawful church leaders.

However, this direction should not be sexist, patriarchal, immune to correction from keener perceptions of what the "mind of Christ" that Paul trumpeted requires. Women trying to lead consecrated lives should enjoy the full confidence of church leaders, as should men. The principle of subsidiarity dear to the Catholic ethical and political tradition should obtain for women as much as men. This principle has it that decisions should be taken at the most local level possible—as close as possible to the people whom the decisions affect most directly. This shows a sublime common sense. Certainly local people can profit from the detached, sometimes more objective views of outsiders. Certainly in the church the universal good is a powerful factor. But many matters quite important for daily life—dress, customs for prayer, housing, relations with laity, types of apostolic work—can only be decided wisely by the people immersed in them, informed about them by having seen them, felt them, on the spot, in action.

As well, in every culture there are things that women do, problems that women face that men, as outsiders, can only guess at. For men not to trust women to handle these things as they see best is for men to show themselves as patronizing in the extreme. So, in the spirit of Galatians 3:18 again, there should be no male or female in the matter of the autonomy proper to religious. Women should have the measures of self-determination available to men.

### 85. What would a liturgy for women ideally feel like?

It would feel like the good news of Christ in feminist garb, anointing the aspirations of women to a humanity equal to that to which men can aspire. Admittedly, one can hear the current Christian liturgies as offering the license to feel in this way, but only by filtering out much patriarchal static. The core message of the gospel certainly is not sexist. Women are as much children of God, candidates for forgiveness, healing, and immortal life, as are men. But the cultural patinas laid over the gospel have regularly promoted men over women. Men have been the normative, median sex. Women have constantly lived either on the fringes of saintliness or, at the other extreme, in whoredom. Women have not been considered fit for priestly ordination, in most times and places. They have not become popes and patriarchs. A few have become universal teachers, and many have offered profound spiritual wisdom, but in nothing like the measures that men have achieved such statuses.

A Christian liturgy effective for women would convey that these historical facts need not foreclose women's future. As feminism has raised consciousness of the oppressions that women have suffered, it has asked the churches to repent of their sexist past and grant women complete equality with men. Women constitute the population that Jesus singled out in the beatitudes (Matthew 5) just as much as men. Jesus admitted women to the circles of both discipleship and personal friendship. Feminists argue that Jesus did not make women members of the circle of the twelve because the patriarchal culture of his day made such a move unthinkable. Either Jesus himself did not think of doing this (as fully human, Jesus was limited much as the rest of us always are), or he thought of it and decided it would not be prudent. However, the logic of Jesus' own sense of his mission (see, for example, Luke 4:18–21) runs to the complete liberation of women and so to their full inclusion at all levels of church life.

An effective liturgy would find words, images, gestures, music, dance, readings and more, to symbolize women's complete inclusion. It would feature women leading the ceremony, preaching, ministering to the rest of the community. It would not be separatist, implying that women are a coven set apart within the church. It would not stress past grievances so much as present joys in the experience of the good news of Christ. For once, women might feel that the church, the gospel, divinity itself belonged to them as much as to men. For once, church culture would reflect what feminists take to be authentic church faith.

## 86. How would Christian feminists reform canon law?

Radically. First, they would ask how much law a community that owes its being to the Spirit of God actually needs. Second, they would require that all canons square with the primacy of charity, divine love, in the community of Christ. Third, they would insist on a prejudice in favor of liberty, the principle of subsidiarity, and both the competence and the goodness of individual Christians. Thus, fourth, their theology of law would make it as much advisory as normative. Fifth, they would require that the body of those revising canon law include as many female members as male. Relatedly, they would demand a dialogical, ecological method of determining new laws, such that canons did not descend from the top of an ecclesiastical pyramid as patriarchal edicts but emerged from the patient discernment of truly representative Christians.

It is not hard to defend the proposition that the community of Christ requires laws. Laws are an efficient way of stipulating what behavior a community approves and what it forbids. The history of the church shows more than enough aberration from sound faith and morals to justify such laws. It also shows that canons have never guaranteed either orthodoxy or holiness.

The fact is that nothing but the Spirit of Christ can "guarantee" either orthodoxy or holiness. The church stands or falls by the work of the Paraclete, the Helper and Comforter that Jesus left to continue his mission. This does not mean that members of the church, disciples of Christ, do not have to work with might and main. It does not mean that feminist Christians do not have to labor diligently at church politics. But it does mean that law ought to have a subordinate, second or third-tier place in the schematization of Christian existence.

Karl Rahner has said that the cardinal dogmas are three: Trinity, Incarnation, and Grace. These are the crux, the defining inmost structure, of Christian existence. One can say that scripture and sacrament express them. One can also say that popes and curias, ethical codes and canon laws, ought mainly to serve to promulgate this defining inmost structure—to forward the life of union with the Trinity, in Christ, through God's grace. Christian feminists aware of the actual proportions of the message and life that Jesus bequeathed them will stand free of canon law psychologically. It will seem to them as good or bad as the degree to which it promotes honesty and love—the life of God in all of Christ's followers.

## 87. Is there a distinctly feminist prayer?

No, at least not at the present time. One can speculate that most feminists will strike certain notes in their Christian prayer, but inasmuch as the Holy Spirit is the prime teacher of prayer, feminists must leave great freedom for all Christians to pray as the Spirit moves them to do. Among the notes that I find most congenial are praying with the confidence of a daughter who feels beloved by a splendid parent, praying for real change in this world of space and time, blood and pain, and asking for a proper freedom from worry, a proper sense that though we should love life as a wonderful gift of God, we have here on earth no lasting city.

The confidence of a child who feels beloved by a splendid parent knows few bounds. The child can climb on the parent's lap when small, go to the parent for emotional support when mature, commiserate with the parent over the ills of the world when aging. Just as the child can be female or male, so can the image of the parent. The child, whether young or old, imagines the parent to be completely interested, wholly on her or his side. There is no possibility that the parent might not accept the child, might find the child disgusting. There is every assumption that what bothers the child bothers the parent.

The child accepts the mystery of having an all-powerful parent who seems unable or unwilling to prevent horrible evils. Often this mystery is hard to accept, but the parent provides sufficient strength, enough comfort, to make acceptance possible. Jesus, the best of the parent's children, went to a horrible death. The parent did not save the best representative of our race. So, most likely the parent will not spare us, for reasons that the parent must find good.

Hurt, crying, lacerated, feminists have to take their grievances, show their wounds, to their parental God. They cannot hide even their most shameful wounds, those produced by their own sins. Remembering the parable of the prodigal son, and perhaps translating it into a story of a prodigal daughter, they have to make their own Jesus' unqualified assertion that our parental God always "prevents" us—is out of the house and onto the path at the first glimpse of our homecoming.

Second, I suspect that Christian feminist prayer fittingly focuses on asking for real change in this fractured world of space and time. Certainly there are moments in all prayer when the Spirit moves us simply to praise God for his or her own splendor. That God is God is the great wonder and foundation of our lives. But the prayer of Jesus encourages us to ask God without ceasing for the things we need. It sanctions prayer of petition as a regular way of expressing our faith that God is real, alive, making a difference, perhaps even suffering alongside us. So we have to remind God of all the children who are starving, in all the diverse ways that human sin has made possible. We have to remind God of all the people who are lonely, going mad, slated to die this day, wracked with pain, promoting still more sin, ruining the environment, abusing women and children—in a word, suffering and causing others to suffer.

This "remind" is a fiction, of course, because faith says that God knows our needs before we even express them, just as faith says that God cares for our well-being more than we do ourselves. But it is good for us to remind God, as it is good for us to haggle with God, imitating Abraham and Job. It is how we invite God to care for us.

Still, after such an exercise, such a way of trying to engage both

God and ourselves with the needs of the world, we ought to imitate Jesus on the cross, commending our spirits into God's keeping. What matters is not that our will be done but that God's will triumph, on earth as it does in heaven. Inasmuch as feminists believe ardently that God's will for them is justice, they can commend their spirits to God and pray the "Our Father" as enthusiastically as any other believers.

Last, I find myself praying for the peace that comes from a proper, nonescapist realization that heaven is my only true home and earth is no lasting city. Every night that I come home battered by human stupidity, I find this peace threatened. Even when young I never put all my trust in princes or princesses, but nowadays I put nearly no trust there. Year by year, it becomes clearer that work for social justice—in my case through fidelity to my vocation as a teacher in higher education—makes progress painfully slowly and precariously. The "sin of the world" is massive, an inertial force moving as irrestibly, it often seems, as the glaciers or the flow of lava down a mountain side.

My faith tells me that I should not fear this massive evil, because Jesus has overcome the world, but my prayer often amounts to, "Lord, I believe; help thou my unbelief." I need the assurance that all the workaday toil I see going for naught will cease one day in a heavenly sabbath. I want the reassertion of the definitive, eschatological character of the salvation that Jesus has accomplished. And I would have every woman who ever slumped with weariness, ever cried with frustration and near-despair, find in the Spirit of Christ precisely this reassertion: nothing is for naught. God treasures the smallest cup of cold water given in her name.

## 88. How can wives be subject to their husbands?

Some of the women slumped with weariness feel themselves nearly defeated by this question. Their husbands have brought them great grief. They have to scrape the bottom of their faith to believe that their husbands have not ruined their lives, remembering the Pauline assurance (Romans 8:38–39) that nothing can separate them from the love of God in Christ Jesus. Women abandoned by their husbands, battered by their husbands, hurt to the quick by their husbands' infidelity, or just worn down by the constant work of trying to be good wives and mothers, can find a great resentment growing. They have been subject to their husbands. Their lives have been directed by his wants and needs, much more than their own. They have been the second sex, the sex seldom receiving a fair shake.

The biblical injunction (Ephesians 5:22, see also Titus 2:2–5) that women be subject to their husbands clearly comes from a patriarchal culture in which the subordination of women to men was assumed. It was one of the rules for good household order that was taught in the Hellenistic world in which the deutero-pauline authors lived. Nowadays, this strikes feminists as incompatible with the liberation at the core of the gospel. Wives can only be subject to their husbands as their husbands are subject to them. In Christ there is no male or female, no superior or inferior. Deference, humility, and submission all ought to flow along a two-way street.

But many women still do not experience this. Many households have a simpler traffic pattern: the male "head" commands and the subject wife and children obey, in varying degrees, with various rebellions. So feminist Christians argue that women cannot be simpleminded about the injunction to be subject to their husbands. They have to distinguish, mock, debunk, and go through the other exegetical tasks necessary to extract a meaning compatible with their conviction that unless the gospel liberates women to full equality with men it purveys little good news, is terribly hard to embrace.

This difficulty in embracing a sexist gospel is not the scandal that Jesus said is always bound to be. It is not the hard saying that we must lose our lives in order to find them. Rather, it is a plain, very human defect in the minds of some gospel writers. In the concrete, a given woman crushed by her subjection can rightly draw strength from associating herself with the scandalous Christ or the biblical command to lose her life, but in itself the sexism that Jewish, Hellenistic, and new Christian patriarchies have imprinted in the New Testament is nothing to defend. Rather, it is something to criticize and reject, even though it can be a source of paradoxical comfort:

the Word of God really has taken flesh and dwelt among us. The gospel really is a thoroughly human affair, right down to ugly warts and warped ideas.

## 89. How should feminists regard divorce?

As a painful failure to achieve an ideal that Jesus sketched (in good measure to liberate women), but also as something that circumstances may make right and necessary. Thus, divorce has nothing singular about it. It is nothing especially sinful, shameful, bound to alienate us from God. It is "merely" another sign of our weakness, sinfulness, constant need of God. It is merely another great stimulus to pray harder and better.

Statisticians tell us that about half the people in the United States who marry nowadays will divorce. Divorce has become commonplace. Nonetheless, divorce remains painful, perhaps especially for women. Beneath the surface even strong feminists can be grieving over the failure of a marriage, the damage they see done to all involved. Marriage is the most intimate human relationship. More than the relation between a parent and child, it exposes us to great hurt. Our spouse is our equal, the one we hoped would become the other half of our self. Our spouse is the one with whom we set out to make a common life, walking all the way to the great darkness of death. With our spouse we hoped to advance toward the abolition of mine and thine that tells us how the divine persons themselves must live. For so lofty a set of ambitions to crash in a welter of accusations, recriminations, bitterness and guilt is not only humiliating but is also a body-blow to our faith.

How can God love us, if the person to whom we entrusted ourselves with fullest nakedness turned aside? How can we love ourselves, if we have proven a terrible failure at the one thing we told ourselves was necessary: finding with another person a love that would justify life and make faith possible? Feminists, like any people of compassion, have to look tenderly, with a desire to comfort, on any people going through such pains. They ought especially to look tenderly on divorced women, because divorce is often an occasion when the oppression of women becomes glaringly obvious.

The majority of women in American society still fear divorce for the insecurity it threatens to visit upon them. They have not been the major breadwinners. They have not had the chance to develop careers parallel to those of their husbands. Even the women who have gotten jobs comparable to their husbands usually feel more responsible for the future of the children than he does. Usually they suspect that in a divorce the children will end up with them and both they and the children will be at the mercy of the father's willingness to provide child support. If it has taken two salaries to keep the family afloat, a divorce leading to the establishment of two separate households threatens to capsize the entire operation. So divorce is financially frightening.

It is also frightening emotionally. What will it mean to be a single parent? What will change in the way that others look at me, in the social patterns that the perceptions of others create? Will I be looked upon by men as fair game, by married women as a threat? Will I ever find a new love, a solution for my loneliness? And how will it go with the church? Will I be able to obtain an annulment to enable me to remarry? Will I find myself cut off from the sacraments? Already I feel a failure. Will my church sharpen this feeling?

Feminists ought to be in the front ranks of those offering divorced women both practical help and emotional support for dealing with questions like these. They ought to be sponsoring support groups, sources of information about resources, new ways to think. Christian feminists ought to be doing this while keeping up the pressure on their churches to help divorced people deal with the religious crisis that divorce always threatens to create. They also ought to keep up the pressure on their churches to deepen their theologies and spiritualities of marriage and communicate them more effectively, so that more marriages can draw on the riches of faith, both at the outset and as the spouses age together.

The great mystery of marriage makes it a symbol of Christ's union with the church, as Christ's union with the church is the expanded context, the superior horizon, within which marriage gains its deepest resonance. When divorce becomes an occasion to ponder this mystery more deeply and realize the grace on which it depends, what seemed like an utter failure may become the occasion for great spiritual growth.

## 90. Is celibacy still viable?

The question requires several distinctions. If "celibacy" refers to the law that all priests in the Roman Catholic Church must abstain from marriage and live chastely, without sexual relations, it appears not to be viable any longer, if it ever was. Failure to find celibacy a positive experience is a major reason why great numbers of priests have recently resigned from the ministry. Failure to find celibacy attractive, persuasive in prospect, is a major reason why great numbers of men otherwise interested in priestly ministry do not present themselves as candidates. The sexual revolution has pulled celibacy down from the superior position it enjoyed in premodern Catholic spirituality. Most people no longer accept the argument that abstention, even so as to present an eschatological sign of the priority of divine grace, is necessarily effective. Sensible people judge the value of a practice by its fruits, its efficacy. The many troubles that celibates have displayed in recent years have given the lie to the argument that abstinence is something intrinsically superior to sexual experience.

On the other hand, if "celibacy" covers the option for virginity as part of a consecrated religious life, whether that laid out by monastic vows or that chosen in another way, then it would be rash to rule celibacy out of court. Celibacy is a charism, a gift of the Holy Spirit. The Spirit gives as the Spirit wishes. The numerous religious people who seem to flourish through celibacy show that the Spirit is still giving this gift. They challenge the aggressive assumption of secular people that sexual pleasure is a natural right, perhaps even a natural need, and so that celibacy is unnatural, bound to make a person neurotic. They show that celibacy can free people for mobile, unusually generous and self-sacrificing service of others.

Overall, then, celibacy seems to have failed as a law, an imperative imposed from without, but not to have died as a charism that the Spirit may give to a few people chosen to spread the gospel in unusual freedom.

## 91. How should feminists regard single lay Christian life?

As a valid, usually underappreciated vocation. For many centuries, Christian spirituality attended only to two vocations, religious life and married life. Religious life held pride of place. It was the life of "the evangelical counsels," supposedly established by Jesus himself as the more perfect way to be a disciple. Married life was such a usual and normal way of life that it was bound to receive considerable attention from church leaders, even though a great deal of such attention was grudging, condescending, and ill-informed. If male superiors often botched the job of directing female religious, they did a worse job of helping other people, especially married women. By refusing to let women speak for themselves, to rule their own domains, church leaders regularly lost most of their credibility with married people.

Single lay people were the poor relations, receiving only the scraps of attention left over after the care and feeding passed out to religious and married people. Single lay people were "bachelors" or "old maids"—pejorative terms both. They were expected to remain virginal, and they were most praised for helping their parents, or contributing to the support of the church, or in general not making a fuss. Their single status often was laid at their own door: they were too unattractive or unambitious to garner a spouse.

Feminists nowadays deal with social patterns that show a proliferation of single women, many of them heading up households. Many single women over thirty-five have despaired of ever finding a suitable man. Many divorced women or unmarried mothers have decided that life alone without an abusive man is preferable to marriage to one. These women need considerable support, and many are finding it in feminist circles. Women's groups, meeting to discuss a great variety of topics, allow tens of thousands of single females to realize that they are not completely alone, that their problems are not unique, that with humor and realism they can compose lives of great significance.

## 92. Are women the helpmates of men?

In fact, a great many women are, though no woman ought to accept "helpmate" as her primary characterization, something that she is ordained to be simply by issuing from her mother as a female.

A great many wives and women-friends allow men to function much better than they would be able to do on their own. So do numerous mothers and sisters, secretaries and assistants. Women care for vast amounts of scut work, background labor, details that are crucial to the grand enterprises for which men usually take the credit. Women do not head corporations as frequently as men do, and men do not staff secretarial pools as frequently as women do. If this auxiliary, ancillary status is what "helpmate" conjures up, it is a description of women's situation that is both accurate and depressing.

The biblical figure of helpmate, from the creation account of Genesis 2, has strong patriarchal overtones, but also a touch of romance, tenderness, and delight. Adam, the first man, the trial run at making a human being, is lonely, incomplete. It is not good for him to be alone. So, God makes him a mate, to complete him. Male and female God reconfigures humanity, the image of divinity that God has decided to place at the pinnacle of creation. Adam delights in this completer of his humanity. She is just what he was longing for, though unawares. It is unfortunate, from a feminine perspective, that Eve is something of an afterthought, and that she comes from Adam's rib and so seems derivative ("deribative"?).

It is even more unfortunate that the myth of how human misfortune and suffering arose makes her the one seduced by the serpent into beginning the tragic disobedience. Yet one may even read the sequence of the fall with a certain ironic delight: it is typical of human beings to blame their troubles on others. Eve blames the serpent, Adam blames Eve. From the beginning, the relations between the sexes have been a mixture of attraction and mutual misunderstanding.

True to the feminist line I have been hewing throughout this book, I believe that women can only be helpmates to men analogously to the way that men can be helpmates to women. I believe that the marriage of the sexes for which feminists have both to yearn and to labor is one of strict equality. Men ought to help women with women's work, whatever women choose that to be, just as much as women ought to help men. Any subordination of the career, emotional needs, or other aspects of one partner's life to those of the other ought to be worked out through the free discussion of equals, based on who has what talents to offer and what needs to be met. In the best of cases, each looks out for the other more than for him or herself.

### 93. How should feminists think about Eve?

With a proper sophistication. First, they should take her as a figure in a myth, a story set outside historical time for the purpose of explaining basic features of the universal human condition. Eve is the mother of all living things. In the background stands Mother Earth. She is how the biblical writer is imagining the female progenitor standing at the origins of our kind, at a time now out of mind, recoverable only through poetic musing. The biblical poet makes her as clever as Adam, and he or she paints Eve's differences from Adam both attractively and poignantly. If patriarchal biases against women slant the account in Genesis in Adam's favor, the objective strengths of actual women keep the portrait from becoming a cartoon.

Second, Eve has been blamed for precipitating the fall of primal humanity from paradisial grace to a state of alientation from both God and our best human potential. This state Christians call sin, and if they follow St. Augustine they speak of it as a state ("original sin") passed along through procreation, much like a sexually communicated disease. Indeed, many of the fathers of the church turned misogynistic as they commented on Genesis 2, lashing out at Eve as the prototypical female keeping the male from achieving the heights of spiritual prowess that, apart from her, he surely would have gained.

It is obvious that there was no cadre of church mothers available to refute this misogynism and balance the scales. The same patriarchal biases to which misogynistic fathers such as Tertullian, Augustine, Chrysostom, and Jerome gave purple vent determined that women would not be bishops, leading preachers, the writers on whom later generations would cut their theological teeth. Thus, feminist theologians rightly toss out the biases of the church fathers as not worth the time of day. Admittedly, the writings of these men had a great negative influence in later Christian history, but in themselves, as analyses of either actual female human nature or the psychology of sexual relations, they are not worth the parchment on which they were written.

Third, feminists therefore ought to rehabilitate Eve, arguing that she has been slandered down through the ages. The primary representative of female humanity should not have to suffer abuse by being pictured as depraved, a temptress responsible for all human woes, the downfall of noble Adam. She should not be set up as a fall-girl, so that Mary, the Second Eve, can reign as the redeeming Virgin Mother and Queen of Heaven. Rather, she should become our mythical mother and paradigm, whose reputation we set out to recover, as a simple matter of mythological justice and feminist self-defense.

### 94. How can girls love a church that discriminates against them?

More than once I have heard otherwise conservative Catholics, many of them men, say that what opened them to the validity of the charges made by feminist Catholics that their church is now sinfully sexist, was the rejection of their daughters for service at the altar. In the dioceses that forbid girls the right to serve at mass alongside boys, the rejection manifest in this symbolism has moved many people—many girls themselves, and great numbers of their parents —to question deeply the justice, even the common sense, of Catholic officials. Virtually all of these girls and their parents have inferred rather quickly from such a rejection, that women have been forced into a generally subordinate, unequal place in Roman Catholicism.

Rejection for service as altar girls has led to a contemplation of what it means to women that they cannot be priests, and so can never aspire to full spiritual leadership in this church.

The only way that either such girls or their parents can love their sexist church is by gaining a wider understanding of its overall being and function that relativizes its sexist sins. This is possible, and to my mind valid, but not easy. The church is its own greatest enemy in dealing with liberated women. Again and again it shoots itself in the foot. As women repeatedly say, church leaders just don't "get it." They are blind, deaf, stupid about women's complaints, because to see, hear, and understand them would require a whole-sale conversion, from the ways of patriarchy to the standards of Christ's gospel. They hide behind the supposed practice of Jesus and the millennial tradition of treating women as second-rate.

Nonetheless, the church, despite all its insensitivities and sins, is the way that God has chosen to express most clearly the salvation accomplished in Christ. For orthodox Christianity, the only salva-tion there is occurs through the redemptive revelation that came to climax in the death and resurrection of Christ. The only body regu-larly, officially, fully re-presenting this salvation is the community that Jesus begot and continues to rule. Saying this does not deny that many people not explicit members of the church show signs of being taken over by the saving Spirit of Christ. The salvation that Christ accomplished is available in all places and times, even though the institutional church may not be. God goes ahead of the church, offering the divine love to all of humanity. Still, this offer is ecclesial, in that it has a natural bent to incorporate people into the body of Christ. Inasmuch as we love salvation because we understand that it is our reason for being, the only way that our humanity will be healed and fulfilled, we have to love the church and keep faith with it, even when its leaders at times may not keep faith with us but may hurt us through patriarchal follies and sins.

## 95. Must Christian feminist spirituality be ecumenical?

Yes, for two main reasons. First, Christianity itself is ecumeni-cal. When it does not think, act, and pray ecumenically it fails its

Lord (see John 17). Second, feminism is ecological, relational, concerned to build bridges, spin webs. For it to hunker down in any one spiritual tradition would be for it to contradict the mindset of its best spokespersons.

Christian ecumenism is well under way, though also stalled unconscionably. In actual practice, educated Christians read, pray, and work together across denominational lines. Scholarship is ecumenical, as are many programs for social welfare. Spiritual writers appeal to those outside their own congregations, and most people seriously interested in spirituality read authors from different churches. Only the most fearful Christians do not see a great potential enrichment in learning about other spiritual traditions.

Roman Catholics, for example, ought to find in the Eastern Orthodox veneration of icons much stimulus for their own spiritual imaginations, as they ought to find a similar stimulus in black Baptist interpretations of scripture or charismatic experiences of the Spirit. Ecumenism and catholicity are two sides of the same coin. Those wanting to live according to the whole (in a "catholic" fashion) have to be open to ecumenism (the entire known world of, in this case, Christian religious experience). In this light, the failure of church leaders to solve the political problems blocking a complete reunion of the separated churches smacks of bureaucracy, self-service, typically male intransigence, and several other species of unbelief.

Much the same applies for the feminist thought that attracts me. If feminists close down their sympathies, refusing to reach out to men, or to deal with the problems of women outside their own culture, they default on some of their own best instincts. Women often pride themselves on being the nurturers, those who conceive life and bring it up with passionate commitment. Spirituality is concerned with conceiving spiritual life and bringing it up with passionate commitment. Ideally, it is concerned about the spiritual development (the religious, or even simply human progress) of all the people it encounters. Feminist spirituality can only do this if its bias is ecumenical—if it responds to truth, beauty, wisdom, need, petition, and hurt wherever it finds them.

### 96. Do women have special ties to death?

Yes, this seems to be the case, when one consults the historical record of the religious symbols surrounding female sexuality. First, we note that the ancient Mother Goddess was not only the source of life, the womb, but also the one to whom life returned when it was finished, the tomb. Mother Earth performed both functions. Second, we note that women have traditionally been the keeners and buriers in most societies. At death, they have unbound their hair, gnashed their teeth, scratched their faces, followed the dead body in procession ululating. They have anointed the bodies of the dead and prepared them for burial, just as his female friends anointed Jesus. They have been the *pietas,* receiving back the bodies of all the children who died too young.

Certainly, when humanity consisted mainly of hunters and gatherers, men held the killing power and women the power of life, but this did not mean women's separation from death. Each month women issued forth blood, the horrifying sign of mortality. Each month they had to go into seclusion, lest this power of death and life conflict with the vitality of the tribe's men and the resultant, confluent stream be polluted. In traditional Asian thought the Great Goddess can take the form of Kali, mistress of death, time as the devourer of all that exists discretely, moment by moment, always portending its own demise.

In myriad ways, therefore, women have had special associations with death, and ideally feminists would criticize each of them, to assure that they not become negative and work beneath the psychic surface to the harm of women's spiritual development.

### 97. Why is Mary Magdalene a heroine to Christian feminists?

Several reasons come to mind. First, she was so intimate with Jesus that he appeared to her first after the resurrection, commissioning her to spread the news of his rising to the apostles. Second, as developed in Christian legend and art, she was a passionate soul, so in love with her Lord that she could throw dignity to the winds and

publicly anoint his feet, drying them with her own hair. Third, identified with the Mary sister to Martha, she came to stand for the
contemplative life, which Jesus called the better part: paying more
attention to him, when he is present, than to practical tasks that will
always press upon us. Fourth, identified with the woman out of
whom Jesus had cast seven devils, the Magdalene stood for the
former sinner so grateful for forgiveness that she burned with a love
that those always righteous could barely comprehend. Thus, Mary
Magdalene became a rich, compound figure, full of angles and
meanings of central interest to women.

In medieval European art, Mary Magdalene often appears
counterposed to the Virgin. Where the Virgin is serene and sorrowful, draped in dark colors, the *Mater Dolorosa* or gentle Madonna,
Magdalene is often fiery, a redhead looking slightly wild, an *apas-
sionata*. Together, the two figures of the Virgin and the Magdalene
compose a complete feminine psychology. Christian feminists tend
to respond to this completeness with much relish, for they realize
that women ought never to be confined to stereotypes—either all
gentle or all fiery, either all sorrowful or all exultant with love. The
wonderfully wide range of female emotions and gifts deserves full
play, a complete unfurling. Mary Magdalene helps Christian feminists anchor this conviction in the New Testament itself.

## 98. What is womanchurch?

No doubt the word carries slightly different connotations for
different users, but my sense is that it names a gathering of women
who have drawn aside from the mainstream to rest, recuperate, and
prepare themselves for a future living of their Christian faith that
will be healthier, because better prepared to counter the noxious
influences of ecclesiastical patriarchalism. Some proponents of
womanchurch seem to think separatistically, as though women
ought to draw aside, not simply as a temporary tactic, but for the
long haul. Others speak in this recuperative, temporary, therapeutic
way that I have sketched. All, however, seem motivated by an experience of having found the mainstream church, the ordinary parish,

unbearable. Not finding nourishment there, indeed often coming home with their wounds reopened rather than healed, they have decided that it is time for a dramatic change.

Gathering with other women, finding comfort with like minds and hearts, feminists enthusiastic about womanchurch report worshiping God more freely, joyously, than they have usually found possible. They like the openness to the femininity of God that most womanchurches foster. They love the intuitive understanding, the not needing to spell everything out laboriously, that a sisterhood provides. They know that most of those with whom they are sharing the circle of worship carry deep, painful scars. They feel extremely grateful that the healing power of the gospel can now reach those scars and rub many of them out.

I fear any sort of separatism, thinking it opposed to the catholicity at the core of Jesus' message. I think that the Christian table ought to be open to all who seek the nourishment of Christ's body and blood. So while I can accept womanchurch as a temporary strategy, any suggestion that it should become even semi-permanent seems to me to tend toward schism. We Christians have always divided too quickly. We have always been slower to listen to the imperatives of John 17 than to our own hotheadedness.

To split and run when things are not going one's own way is not a sign of heroism. Certainly, times can come when, God help us, we can do no other, if we are to honor our consciences and save our faith. But these times are rare. Generally, we ought to avoid self-dramatization like the plague and make sure that we do not talk ourselves into spiritual ghettos, emotional cul-de-sacs. Compared to the will of our Lord that we be one, our own egos are not all-important. So I pray that womanchurch will not turn out to be simply another protest that began well but then withered, because it drew apart from the single vine.

## 99. What repentance do feminists ask of the church?

First, that its leaders admit the sinfulness of sexism and vow to root it out of both church teaching and church practice. Second, that it make reparation to women by adopting programs that promote the aspirations of women though a version of affirmative action.

Sexism is a sin, regardless of the slowness of church leaders (for example, many Roman Catholic bishops) to acknowledge this fact. A sin is any moral evil—any wrongdoing that is culpable. Discriminating against women is doing wrong. Any discrimination that is conscious, deliberate, stemming from a closure of mind and heart, a failure of conscience, is immoral—doing wrong culpably. Thus, it is sinful. Perhaps one can say that many traditional acts and policies that discriminated against women arose from the mores of the day and were not very conscious or deliberate. Today, however, one can hardly advance such a defense with a straight face. The Catholic Church is well aware of balanced feminist critiques of its teaching and practice, both past and present. For it not to admit the sinfulness of its traditional subjugation of women and repent is for it to compound its wrongdoing, deepen its guilt.

It would be a fine beginning for church leaders simply to admit their past failures and apologize to the many women the church has wronged, but this would not be enough. To show itself fully repentant, converted completely to the good news of Christ, the church would also have to establish affirmative policies aimed at bringing women into the mainstream of ecclesiastical power and responsibility as quickly as possible.

The great symbol and practical mechanism for doing this is admitting qualified women to priestly ordination—opening the inner sanctums. With this single stroke, a thousand taboos and obstacles would fall away. The full church would gain access to perhaps twenty-five percent more talent (the half that women now cannot offer). Half the church's membership could breathe deeply for the first time, finally freed of the yoke of second-class citizenship.

Admitting qualified women to orders would not be a panacea. A great many problems would remain. Women are no less sinful, imperfect, in need of continual repentance than men. But finally the church would be rid of its patriarchal soul. Finally it would not be burdened with the great lie that men are necessarily more competent in matters of faith than women, necessarily better vicars of

Christ, shepherds of the faithful, mediators between sinful humanity and the all-holy, all-merciful God.


## 100. What would you do if you were made pope?

Immediately begin this program of practical repentance. I can see nothing more important for the future prospering of the Catholic Church, because I can see nothing targeting a more universal good. Not only would half the population of both the churched and the unchurched receive an engraved invitation to come into full, actual equality with the other half, a dozen major reforms would immediately leap onto the church's agenda, actually becoming possible for the first time.

For example, we could get fully to work on the new spirituality that both women and men require. We could attack and perhaps solve once and for all the bugaboo of sexuality, which has poisoned the theology of marriage, canon law, religious life, the priesthood, and virtually every other aspect of Catholic culture. We could hear the full voice to which we need to listen if we are to get in our sights such problems as war and the establishment of social justice on an international scale. We could attack the problems of world hunger and world health as a church that knew from the inside, out of its own experience, that women hold half the resources for nourishing God's people and healing their hurts. On and on it could go.

If I were made pope, I would start with an exegesis of both scripture and tradition that took Galatians 3:18 as, not a proof text, but a two-edged sword, cutting to the joint and marrow of both past sexism and future egalitarianism. I would urge an exegesis that overlooked none of the liabilities in the received New Testament, tainted as it was by patriarchal biases, but that also overlooked none of its universal power. Christian revelation has always been good news for women as much as for men. The blunting of its force by patriarchal abuses of women has never snuffed out its light. The light has kept shining, even in the darkness of sexism, and that darkness has not comprehended the gospel—not understood it, and not wrapped it up. Making women fully equal with men in the one society that the pope can influence directly and mightily would let the light shine freely, uninhibited by the demons of clerical misogynism. That could make the church's teaching dazzling indeed: a light for the revelation of the Gentiles and the glory of God's people everywhere.


**101.  How ought readers finally to think about women's rights?**

This question offers us a chance to end on a positive note. Readers ought finally to think that women's rights are the equal of men's, both as important and as directly God's gift. Readers also ought to think that women's rights are not a burden or a cause for dissension so much as a simple expression of women's being, which is beautiful in God's sight.

Women's rights are the equal of the rights of men, because the sexes are similarly human. Both men and women enjoy reason and feeling. Both are children of God, washed clean by the blood of Christ. Women are no brighter than men, but also no more stupid. Women are no holier than men, but also no more sinful. Speaking generally, about women and men as groups, one cannot call either sex the better, the superior in humanity. If it is necessary to make comparisons, the only shrewd procedure is to deal with individuals: Mary is smarter than John, as both her test scores and her bank account show. Sam is nicer than Zelda, as anyone who has done business with both can attest.

Therefore, it is common sense, plain justice, and Christian wisdom wrapped in one to treat men and women as essentially equal. It is the only attitude, posture, judgment that one can call either sane or worthy of Jesus. The basic right that feminism seeks for women is this fundamental fair-dealing. Women deserve no more, and no less, than the dignity and respect commanded by ordinary, representative men. This is hardly a revolutionary, incendiary proposition, and in most quarters it will be received kindly. Where it will not be received kindly one has to speak of sexism, and so of sin, and so of closure to God. Indeed, where the rights that women command are not the equal of the rights of men, one has to call for reform—the "repent and believe in the good news" heralded by Jesus at the outset in the gospel of Mark. But even such a call is more joyous than sad. People who want progress, the triumph of God's reign have to see any challenge to the bastions of sin as a move forward, good innings for Jesus' side.

The second notion advanced at the beginning of this question, that the being of women is beautiful in God's sight, can take us into port. Often being beautiful has been thrown at women like a burden, even a noose. Lamentably, the disorder of our kind, both men and women, regularly makes beauty suspect and pulls it out of joint. So for once we should simply rejoice in the beauty of women, as in the beauty of men, recalling that this is God's doing and we should never cease giving thanks. What would we be, any of us, without the light of our eyes and the air we breathe? What would we be without the beauty of our children, the soft curve of little girls' cheeks? We could not believe in creation—the world as the free gift of God—could we not enjoy such beauty. We could not believe in redemption: what in the world could have seized the heart of God sufficiently? The beauty of the women into whom little girls grow is no accidental feature of the world that Christians cherish. The Madonna and child stand at its very center, where all mortal flesh keeps silence, taken out of itself by their beauty.

Often it is hard to believe that, where sin abounded, grace has abounded the more. Often the proofs that tell the most are small acts of kindness: fresh bread, a cool cloth for a troubled brow. Women, full of grace, have brought forth many such proofs. Down the twisting corridors of history, again and again mothers, sisters and daughters have supplied these. I find their supply no argument that women are the moral betters of men. Equally, though, I find it clear refutation of any argument, explicit or tacit, that women are men's inferiors. The beauty of women in God's sight, which runs to the soul even more than the countenance, ought to lure both men and women to gratitude. It ought to be a great stimulus to faith. Indeed, used judiciously, it could put an end to all further questioning, serving as a quiet, consummating "amen."

*Other Books in This Series*

RESPONSES TO 101 QUESTIONS ON THE BIBLE
by Raymond E. Brown, S.S.

RESPONSES TO 101 QUESTIONS
ON THE DEAD SEA SCROLLS
by Joseph A. Fitzmyer, S.J.

RESPONSES TO 101 QUESTIONS ABOUT JESUS
by Michael L. Cook, S.J.